A Source Book of Racing and Sports Cars

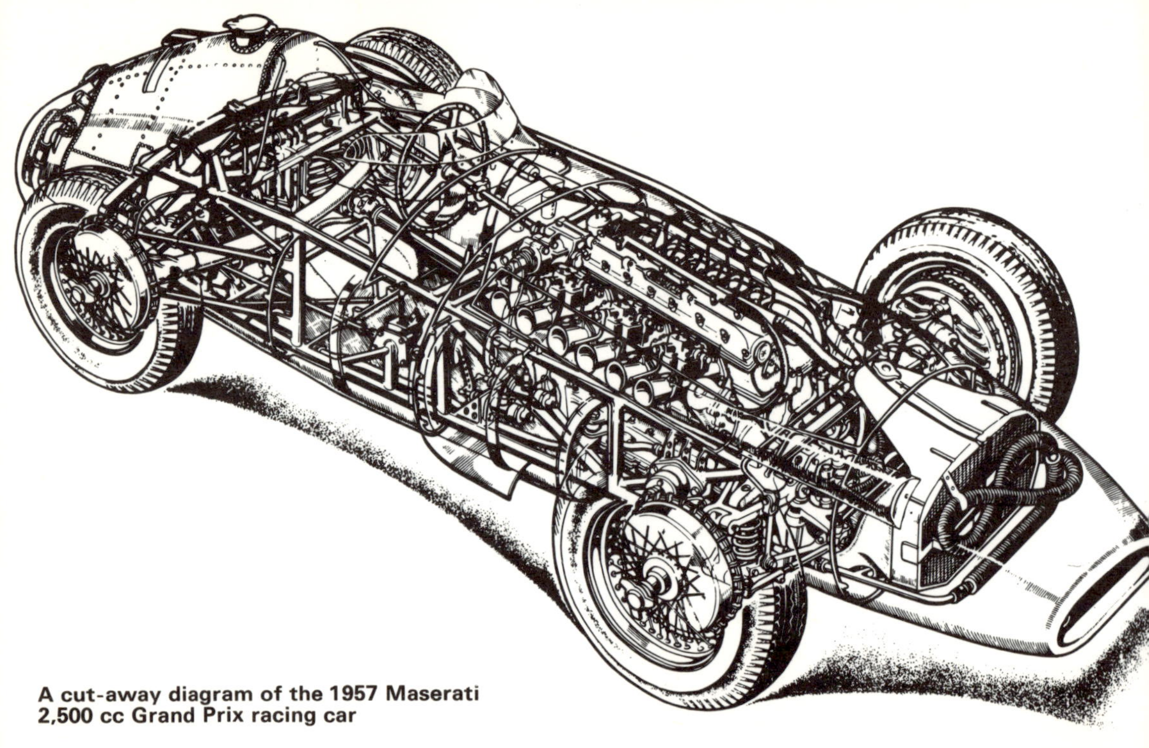

**A cut-away diagram of the 1957 Maserati
2,500 cc Grand Prix racing car**

A Source Book of
Racing and Sports Cars

Compiled and edited by G. N. Georgano

WARD LOCK LIMITED · LONDON

Acknowledgements

The Author and Publishers would like to thank the following for their generous help in providing photographs: *Autocar*, Anthony Blight, Albert R. Bochroch, Bernard Cahier, Geoffrey Goddard, Indianapolis Motor Speedway, Jaguar Cars Ltd, Lotus Cars Ltd, T.A.S.O. Mathieson, *Motor*, National Motor Museum at Beaulieu, Doug Nye, Cyril Posthumus, Royale Racing, Swiss Museum of Transport, Veteran Car Club of Great Britain, Michael Ware.

First published in Great Britain 1973
by Ward Lock Limited, 116 Baker Street,
London, W1M 2BB

Designed by Conal Buck

Text filmset in 7 pt Univers (689)
and printed and bound by
Cox and Wyman Ltd,
London, Fakenham and Reading

For the first few years of motor racing history one could say that there were no racing cars, or with equal accuracy, that almost every motorcar was a potential racer. The Paris–Rouen Trial of 1894 attracted twenty-two assorted entries including a steam bus. This event was not strictly a race as the prizes did not go necessarily to the fastest cars, but in 1895 the first road race was held, from Paris to Bordeaux. Thereafter, for eight successive years, the *Automobile Club de France* organized races of ever increasing length, to Ostend, Amsterdam, Berlin, Vienna and finally, Madrid. The latter race, held in 1903, had to be stopped at Bordeaux because of the shocking number of casualties caused by enormously powerful racing cars travelling at speeds of up to 80 mph on roads carrying everyday traffic. During those eight years of the town-to-town races, the specialized racing car gradually made its appearance, distinguished from its touring counterpart largely by a bigger engine. Design features which later became widespread on touring cars were often pioneered on racing machines, these including four-cylinder engines and inclined steering columns (1898 Panhard), and shock absorbers (1902 Mors). The 1898 Amédée Bollées built for the Paris–Amsterdam Race had streamlined bodies made of aluminium, but it was a long time before the average touring car showed any sign of streamlining. Speeds rose dramatically from the 15 mph average of the winning Panhard in the 1895 Paris–Bordeaux Race to the 65.3 mph maintained by Fernand Gabriel's 80 hp Mors in Paris–Madrid before the race was stopped at Bordeaux.

Up to 1902 all European races had been in a direct line from town to town, but in that year there took place in Belgium the first *Circuit des Ardennes*, in which the contestants had to cover

Land Speed Record I – Camille Jenatzy's *La Jamais Contente*, an electric car which was the first to exceed 100 km per hour (65.79 mph) in April 1899

six laps of a closed circuit. After the disastrous Paris–Madrid Race this became the normal way of organizing races, and has continued to be so to the present day, although now true road circuits are disappearing under pressure from safety-conscious drivers.

A series of races which spanned both open road and circuit racing was that of the Gordon Bennetts, named after the American newspaper proprietor James Gordon Bennett. These were for teams of cars from each country, and the Gordon Bennett Cup was presented to the national team rather than to an individual driver. A maximum of three cars was allowed from each nation, and all parts of the cars had to be made in the country concerned. The design was not included in this stipulation, however, and so one had the situation of Alexandre Darracq entering seven cars in the 1904 race, three from his native France, three Weir-Darracqs from Scotland, and one Opel-Darracq from Germany. As the number of manufacturers who wished to go in for racing grew, the restriction of three cars per country became increasingly irksome. Eliminating Trials were held in Great Britain, France and Germany in which the dozen or so contenders were whittled down to three, but this hardly satisfied the unlucky manufacturers who might have spent thousands of pounds building a team of racing cars which never saw the actual circuit. In 1906 the Gordon Bennetts were replaced by a new race organized by the *Automobile Club de France*, to be known as the Grand Prix, and open to as many contestants as wished to take part. The first Grand Prix, which was a two-day event held on a circuit near Le Mans, attracted thirty-two competitors, mainly from France, although later Grands Prix became more international. Regulations varied from year to year as the organizers strove to find a formula which would encourage the development of safe cars while, at the same time, giving entertaining racing to the public. The 1906 regulations simply stipulated a maximum weight limit of 1,000 kilograms, but later events restricted fuel consumption (1907 and 1913), piston area (1908), width (1912) and engine capacity (1914). After World War I engine capacity became the most widely used formula, and so it has remained up to the present day.

During the period of which we have been speaking, the sports car did not really exist as a separate type. The motorist who wanted a fast car for road use generally bought a superannuated racing car, or simply the chassis of a powerful touring car such as the 60 hp Mercedes, on which he mounted a light two-seater body. At that time the same chassis would serve for a touring limousine or a fast roadster, combining the virtues of present-day cars as different as a Rolls-Royce Phantom VI and a Lamborghini Miura. The sports car as such only appeared when manufacturers began to develop engines whose high performance owed more to design than to sheer size. The earliest sports cars such as the 1908 Prince Henry Horch and 1910 Prince Henry Vauxhall and Austro-Daimler were not large by the standards of the day, and in each case the makers' range included cars which were larger but of lower performance. Improvements which helped to give the new cars more power per litre included overhead valves which gave better breathing and overhead camshafts which eliminated the long pushrods associated with side camshafts and ohv. Aluminium pistons as used by W. O. Bentley in the racing DFPs he developed in 1914, permitted a higher piston speed.

These improvements in design were also found on Grand Prix cars during the period 1912 to 1914, and were demonstrated to great effect in the victory of the 1912 Peugeot over much larger, more old-fashioned cars. The Peugeot was one of

Land Speed Record II – The first car to exceed 100 mph was Rigolly's 100 hp Gobron-Brillié which did 103.55 mph in 1904

the milestone designs of motor racing history in that its rivals had to copy many of its features if they were to remain competitive. These features included inclined overhead valves (four per cylinder) operated by twin overhead camshafts, and monobloc casting of the engine. A later improvement found on many of the 1914 Grand Prix cars, though not on the winning Mercedes, was that of front-wheel brakes.

The best-known early American races were those for the Vanderbilt Cup. This was presented by William K. Vanderbilt Jr for national teams of up to five cars each. In the first three races, held from 1904 to 1906, European cars predominated, for although American manufacturers built some highly interesting and unconventional machines such as the V-4 front-wheel-drive Christie and the straight-8 air-cooled Franklin, European experience told, and Europe had the better drivers. In 1908 America had her revenge when 23-year-old George Robertson drove a Locomobile to victory over the best that Europe could offer. American racing received a great boost with the building in 1909 of the Indianapolis Motor Speedway. This $2\frac{1}{2}$-mile oval track was never as widely used as was Britain's Brooklands, partly because the owners felt that too many races would reduce attendance in the long run. In 1909 and 1910 a number of short races were held, but 1911 saw the first of the 500 mile events, held then and ever since at the end of May, on Memorial Day. Indianapolis was a brick track, but from 1910 to 1930 a great deal of American racing took place on board tracks, one-mile and two-mile ovals built of long planks of wood, and steeply banked. Among the most famous of the board tracks were those at Sheepshead Bay, Long Island, Union-town, Pennsylvania, and Beverly Hills, California. There were also dirt tracks and a few road courses such as Corona, California. Thus there was much more racing taking place each year in America than in Europe, and a driver could build up points towards the American Automobile Association Championship. In Europe there were only the Grands Prix and the Sicilian Targa Florio, together with a few races for smaller cars, and there was no official Grand Prix Drivers' Championship until 1950.

After World War I the number of European races began to increase, and countries other than France organized Grands Prix. Up to 1914 there had been no need to talk about the 'French Grand Prix' because there were no others, but in 1921 came the first Italian Grand Prix, followed in 1925 by the Belgian, and in 1926 by the German Grand Prix. Front-wheel brakes were universal on the post-war Grand Prix cars, and a new development was the straight-8 engine. This was seen on the Ballots, Sunbeams, Fiats and Duesenbergs, and seemed to be the coming trend, but the smaller cars of 1922 and 1923 had only six cylinders. Superchargers, to force the mixture into the cylinders at a greater than atmospheric pressure, first appeared on the 1923 Grand Prix Fiats, and soon became widespread on racing and sports cars. The Grand Prix formula had progressively reduced the capacity of engines, from 3 litres in 1921 to 2 litres in 1922 to 1925, and $1\frac{1}{2}$ litres in 1926 and 1927. In the late 1920s Grand Prix racing was in the doldrums, and it was not unusual for stripped sports cars such as the Mercedes-Benz SSK to run alongside Bugatti and Alfa Romeo Grand Prix cars. Various weight limits were in force from 1928 to 1930, but for the next three years a *formule libre* prevailed, in which cars of any size or weight could compete. At this time Maserati came on to the field as a new make to be reckoned with, and competed against Bugattis and Alfa Romeo's Tipo 2600B and 2900B. These three makes might have dominated Grand Prix racing indefnitely, had not Adolf Hitler chosen motor racing as one of the best forms of propaganda for his new National Socialist régime in Germany. The result of this was that two firms, Mercedes-Benz and the new combine, Auto Union, were heavily subsidized to build teams of world-beating cars, which they did magnificently. First to appear was the Mercedes-Benz W25, whose 3,360 cc engine developed 354 bhp, about 100 bhp more than the Alfa Romeo of the period. The Mercedes' handling was greatly aided by independent suspension of all wheels. The Auto Union was a much more revolutionary design, for the engine had 16 cylinders and was mounted behind the driver. Although larger, at 4,360 cc, it was not so powerful as the Mercedes, and on the whole the rear-engined cars did not enjoy the outstanding success of their rivals, who dominated motor racing from 1934 until 1939.

The sports car really came into its own during the twenty years between the wars. From the handful of fast tourers available in 1914 the range extended until, by 1925, there were sporting cars in almost every price range, and made in every motor manufacturing country. The world's best-known sports car race, the Le Mans 24 Hours, was first held in 1923. The rules demanded a full four-seater touring car in road trim (for entries of over 1,100 cc; smaller cars needed to have only two seats). Other events which encouraged sports cars were the Touring Car Grands Prix, held on the eve of the French Grand Prix from 1922 to 1925 inclusive, and 24-hour races at Spa in Belgium and San Sebastian in Spain. Gradually, two types of sports car emerged, the small two-seater in which France excelled, and the larger four-seater typified by the 3-litre Bentleys and Sunbeams, and the French Chenard-Walcker and Lorraine-Dietrich. The small sports car, of which the Amilcar and Salmson were the best-known, brought sports motoring to a new public, selling as they did for between £250 and £285. The factory-prepared sports Austin Seven cost only £175, the same price as the 1929 MG Midget.

Developments pioneered on Grand Prix cars soon found their way to production sports cars; these included front-wheel brakes, a novelty in 1919 but standard wear on practically all cars eight years later, overhead valve engines, operated at first by pushrods and later by one or two overhead camshafts, and superchargers. Beaded-edge high-pressure tyres gave way to wider, lower pressure, balloon tyres. Following the adoption of independent front suspension on Grand Prix cars, this feature was gradually adopted by sports car makers of the 1930s, Alvis being the pioneer in Great Britain with their 1928 front-wheel drive car which in fact used independent rear suspension as well. The traditional British sports car stuck to beam axle, semi-elliptic front suspension until after World War II, but on the Continent such makers as Alfa Romeo, Delahaye, BMW and Mercedes-Benz were all turning to independent suspension of the rear wheels as well as the front.

The Hitler war disrupted the world's motor industry to an even greater extent than its predecessor, but surprisingly motor racing started up again very quickly, the first post-war event being held in the Bois de Boulogne, Paris, in September 1945. All the cars, of course, were pre-war machines. The same situation obtained during 1946, but for 1947 a new Grand Prix formula was announced. This imposed a capacity limit of $1\frac{1}{2}$ litres for supercharged, and $4\frac{1}{2}$ litres for unsupercharged cars, an equivalence which proved remarkably successful as the two types of car were very evenly matched. Until 1951 the $1\frac{1}{2}$-litre supercharged machines represented by Alfa Romeo and Ferrari had the edge on the larger machines, but the advent of the $4\frac{1}{2}$-litre Ferrari with the ability to complete a race without refuelling, combined with Alfa Romeo's with-

Land Speed Record III – The first car to exceed 200 mph was Sir Henry Segrave's 1,000 hp Sunbeam which did 203.79 mph in 1927

drawal from racing, marked a dramatic change, and the supercharged car disappeared from the Grand Prix scene. The 1954 formula reduced the size of engine in both categories, to $2\frac{1}{2}$ litres for unsupercharged, and only 750 cc for supercharged cars. Only one make attempted to build supercharged cars in 1954, the French DB company, but they had no success with them.

Two new formulae came into existence in the post-war period, Formula 2 which was for 2-litre unsupercharged cars, and Formula 3 for 500 cc cars, powered mostly by single-cylinder motorcycle engines. This had begun in England in 1946, and was recognized by the FIA as an international formula four years later. Formula 3 provided very exciting sport for both drivers and spectators for several years. It proved a valuable training ground for young drivers, and among the Formula 3 boys who later achieved fame at the wheel of larger machinery were Stirling Moss, Jack Brabham and Stuart Lewis-Evans. Nearly all Formula 3 cars were rear-engined, and all successful makes were British. By far the greatest number of victories went to Cooper, but Kieft had a short run of successes, especially when Stirling Moss drove for them in 1951 and 1952. Disappointed at their failure to make any impression in Formula 3, the

Italians introduced Formula Junior in 1958. This allowed production engines of up to 1,100 cc, thus making use of the Fiat 1100 engine. Within a year or so, over a dozen Italian firms built Formula Junior cars, mostly front-engined, of which Stanguellini and Taraschi were the most successful. But the British manufacturers turned to this Formula also, and soon rear-engined Lotus and Lola Formula Juniors were beating the Italians at their own game. The old 500 cc Formula 3 lapsed, but the name was revived in 1964 for cars of 1,000 cc or under. This remained in force until January 1971, when the limit was raised to 1,600 cc, but only production engines with a maximum of four cylinders were allowed.

The $2\frac{1}{2}$-litre Formula 1 lasted from 1954 to 1960. Most cars of this era were relatively simple in design; the complex $1\frac{1}{2}$-litre supercharged BRM gave way to a 4-cylinder $2\frac{1}{2}$-litre car, while the most successful car at this time was the 6-cylinder Maserati 250F, again an unsophisticated design. The same could not be said of the Mercedes-Benz W196 with straight-8 engine, desmodromic valve gear and fuel injection, but the German company has always tended to make dramatic gestures on the motor racing scene. Unlike those of many other manufacturers, these gestures nearly always pay off. In 1957 there appeared among the conventional front-engined cars a 4-cylinder 2-litre machine from the small British firm of Cooper, which had its engine behind the driver. With these cars Stirling Moss and Maurice Trintignant won the Argentine and Monaco Grands Prix respectively in 1958. The engine was later enlarged to 2.2 litres, and in 1959 to a full $2\frac{1}{2}$ litres, making the Cooper the first rear-engined Grand Prix car of the post-war era. With Jack Brabham as driver they won the Manufacturers' Championship in 1959, and set a fashion for Formula 1 design which was copied with remarkable speed by all other competitors. The year 1960 was a transitional period, but by 1961 the front-engined Formula 1 car had completely disappeared, along with similar designs in other formulae. Rear-engined dominance became complete when the American USAC Championship cars which ran at Indianapolis and other circuits also became rear-engined in the mid-1960s. Today, only the very simplest racing cars competing in Clubman's Formula still keep their engines ahead of the driver.

In an effort to reduce speeds and promote safety, the Formula 1 was reduced to $1\frac{1}{2}$ litres in 1961, and this limit remained until 1965. It was then replaced by a 3-litre Formula which is still in force at the time of writing and seems likely to remain so for some time. A wide variety of cars has been built for this formula, using either space-frame or monocoque construction, and engines of V-8, V-12, flat-12 or H-16 layout. The most successful has been the V-8, particularly the Ford-based Cosworth unit which has been used by Lotus, McLaren, March, Matra and Tyrrell, as well as other less successful makers. A feature of recent years has been the increasing importance of commercial sponsorship, so that cars run in the colours of cigarette or perfume makers instead of the national colours of old, and in some cases even the makers' name becomes lost, so that a Lotus becomes a John Player Special and a March an STP Oil Treatment Special.

Apart from the old-established formulae, a wide variety of other classes of racing has appeared over the past ten years. This includes Formula 5000 (known as Formula A in America) for cars with production engines of up to 5 litres. These cars are similar in design to those of Formula 1, and their large engines develop approximately the same power, but their greater weight keeps performance below that of the 3-litre cars. Two formulae sponsored by manufacturers are Formula Ford and Formula Vee (Volkswagen) for cars

Land Speed Record IV – The present holder is Gary Gabelich's *Blue Flame* which reached a speed of 622.41 mph in October 1970

powered by 1,600 cc Ford or 1,300 cc Volkswagen engines (1,600 cc in Formula Super Vee), and these have become very popular on both sides of the Atlantic. For enthusiasts with little money there is Formula 750, originally for Austin Seven engines, but now mainly using Reliant units, Formula 1200 (Ford engines) and Clubman's Formula for sports cars in the 1,000 and 1,500 cc classes, many constructed from kits or home-designed and built. There was also the not-very-successful Formula F100 sponsored by Firestone Tyres for 1,300 cc two-seater all-enveloping cars, and Formula Atlantic, an intermediate class between Formulae 2 and 3, derived from the American Formula B.

Sports car racing was slower to get under way than Grand Prix, and the first post-war Le Mans event was not held until 1949, when victory went to a 2-litre V-12 Ferrari. Jaguar's new XK120 had done well in Production Car Races since its introduction in 1948, and in 1951 the Coventry firm prepared a special works team of shortened, tuned XKs, known as the C-type. These began a long series of Jaguar victories at Le Mans; together with their successors the D-types, they won in 1951, 1953, 1955, 1956 and 1957. With Aston Martin's Le Mans victory in 1959 Britain's supremacy seemed as great in sports car racing as it was to become in Formula 1, but it was not to continue for long into the 1960s. No all-British car has won at Le Mans since 1959, and in 1966 only one British car finished, a French-entered Mini-Marcos. As the 1960s passed, the specialized sports car capable of winning at Le Mans or one of the other major sports car events became increasingly divorced from the ordinary road-going car. This trend had been evident before the war, with cars like the tank-bodied 1936 Bugatti which could not be bought by the general public, but at least such cars, and the C-type Jaguars, could be driven to the circuit and home again after the race was over. Increasing competition between makers has led to the so-called sports car becoming a specialized machine, in many cases a thinly disguised Grand Prix car with all-enveloping body and token road equipment. This has been encouraged by FIA regulations which, since 1968, have restricted prototype sports cars to the same engine capacity (3 litres) as Formula 1 cars. However, the 1972 Le Mans race saw larger-engined road-going coupés such as the Ferrari GTB4 and De Tomaso Pantera running in a new GT category, and it is to be hoped that this will be the start of more everyday cars being seen in major sports car competitions.

Maximum Speeds

For many of the racing cars, maximum speeds given are only approximate as the cars have never been officially tested. Also, different gearing makes for variation in speeds between one example and another of the same model of car.

VOITURE DE COURSE DE DIETRICH. CARROSSERIE ROTHSCHILD, APPARTENANT A M. DE PAIVA (Fig. 119)

1898 Amédée Bollée
8 hp racing car

Four of these cars were built to take part in the 1898 Paris–Amsterdam–Paris race. With their torpedo-shaped aluminium bodies, they were the first cars to be specifically designed as competition machines, but they were not as successful as their more conventional-looking rivals. Their best place in Paris–Amsterdam–Paris was Giraud's 3rd, although a Bollée later won the less important Paris–Biarritz race. Some replicas were built, both by Bollée at Le Mans and by the German de Dietrich factory at Niederbronn in Alsace. The photograph shows one of the latter, with special body by Rothschild.

Engine: 2-cyl, 110×160 mm, 3,042 cc. Hot tube ignition, side valves (automatic inlet).
Transmission: 4-speed, shaft drive. 38 mph max.
Chassis: Channel-steel, rear brakes.
Events Won: 1898 Bordeaux–Biarritz race.

1901 Mors

60 hp racing car

For a brief period between 1900 and 1904 Mors was a name to reckon with in motor racing, and the car illustrated won the two main events of 1901, the Paris–Bordeaux and Paris–Berlin races. In the latter, Henri Fournier covered the 687 miles at an average speed of 44 mph running time. The 1902 Mors racing cars were slightly smaller at 9,236 cc compared with 10,087 cc for the 1901 cars, and they were not so successful, their best results being 2nd and 3rd in the Circuit des Ardennes. They were, however, significant in pioneering the use of shock absorbers on racing cars.

Engine: 4-cyl, 130×190 mm, 10,087 cc. Low-tension magneto, side valves (automatic inlet), 60 bhp.
Transmission: 4-speed, chain drive.
Chassis: Channel-steel, rear brakes.
Events Won: 1901 Paris–Bordeaux race, 1901 Paris–Berlin race.

1902   Panhard
70 hp racing car

For the first ten years of racing Panhard was the most successful make, winning major events in 1895, 1896, 1898 and 1899. Challenged by Mors in 1900–01, they came up with a car of over 13½ litres in 1902. The engine had three valves per cylinder, and the unusual suspension had a single transverse leaf in front in place of the two longitudinal ones normally used. In the Paris–Vienna race there were eight 70 hp Panhards, and Henri Farman's finished 2nd overall.
Engine: 4-cyl, 160×170 mm, 13,672 cc. Coil and battery, side valves (automatic inlet), 70 bhp.
Transmission: 4-speed, chain drive. 90 mph.
Chassis: Armoured wood, rear brakes. 8 ft 8 in wheelbase.
Events Won: 1902 Circuit des Ardennes.

1902   Renault
16 hp racing car

Louis Renault's first car appeared in 1898 and used shaft drive to a live rear axle. This was unusual when most makers used chain or belt drive, especially on cars of over 3 litres. 1902 Renaults were the first to use the firm's own engines, and three cars with the new 4-cylinder engine were entered in the Paris–Vienna race. Their weight of 646 kg kept them in the light car class. Marcel Renault won his class, and the whole race.
Engine: 4-cyl, 120×120 mm, 3,758 cc. Coil and battery, side valves (automatic inlet), 30 bhp.
Transmission: 3-speed, shaft drive. 60 mph.
Chassis: Channel-steel, rear brakes.
Events Won: 1902 Paris–Vienna race.

1902 Napier
30 hp racing car

British cars were not at all prominent in the early days of motor racing, and the first two years of Napier's efforts brought very dismal results. For the 1902 Gordon Bennett race S. F. Edge, Napier's famous driver and publicist, entered a 30 hp car, much smaller and more compact than the unwieldy 50 hp 17-litre car which ran unsuccessfully in 1901. After the Panhard driven by René de Knyff had fallen out of the race, Edge went on to win the Cup for Britain, attracting invaluable publicity to his own company and the British motor industry generally. The total cost of the enterprise, including the building of the car, was reckoned to be £1,418, of which £1,200 was recovered later by the sale of the car.
Engine: 4-cyl, 127×127 mm, 6,435 cc. Coil and battery, side valves (automatic inlet), 30 bhp.
Transmission: 3-speed, shaft drive. 65 mph.
Chassis: Channel-steel, rear brakes.
Events Won: 1902 Gordon Bennett race.

1903 Winton
40 hp racing car

Alexander Winton realized early on the publicity value of racing, and entered a car in the original Gordon Bennett race of 1900. The car illustrated was built for the 1903 Gordon Bennett. Both 1903 cars had horizontal engines with identical cylinder dimensions, the 40 hp car with four cylinders and $8\frac{1}{2}$-litres capacity, and the 80 hp with eight cylinders and a 17-litres capacity. They retired during the race, but the larger set various records later in America driven by Barney Oldfield.
Engine: 4-cyl, 133.25×152.4 mm, 8,513 cc. Coil and battery, side valves (automatic inlet), 40 bhp.
Transmission: 2-speed, shaft drive.
Chassis: Wood, rear brakes.
Records: Mile in 55 secs.

1903 Serpollet
racing car

Steam has never been very popular for racing cars, but the steamers of Léon Serpollet achieved considerable fame in the early twentieth century. They had flash boilers and automatic feed of water to the boiler and of oil to the burner. In 1902 Serpollet held the Land Speed Record with a speed of 75.6 mph, and he also entered cars in races such as Paris–Vienna, Paris–Madrid and Circuit des Ardennes.
Engine: 4-cyl, 40 bhp.
Transmission: Shaft drive. 75 mph.
Chassis: Channel-steel, rear brakes.
Records: Land Speed Record – 75.6 mph, Gaillon Hill Climb (1902 car).

1903 Mercedes
60 hp racing car

The 1901 Mercedes 35 hp was a striking breakaway from the high, horseless-carriage type typified by the Panhard. With its honeycomb radiator, mechanically operated inlet valves and selective gearchange it set the pattern for the larger type of car for ten years. The 60 hp car illustrated was a development of the 1901 model, but with overhead inlet valves and a considerably larger engine. Even larger cars of 90 hp were entered for the Gordon Bennett race, but they were destroyed in a factory fire, and Mercedes had to enter some hastily commandeered and stripped 60 hp touring cars. Jenatzy's car won the race, and another 60 hp Mercedes was 5th.

Engine: 4-cyl, 140×150 mm, 9,236 cc. Low-tension magneto, inlet over exhaust, 60 bhp.
Transmission: 4-speed, chain drive. 75 mph.
Chassis: Channel-steel, rear brakes, 275 cm wheelbase.
Events Won: 1903 Gordon Bennett race.
Records: La Turbie Hill Climb.

1904 Wolseley
96 hp racing car

From 1895 to 1905 Wolseley cars were designed by Herbert Austin, and they all had horizontal engines. Austin pursued an ambitious racing programme, entering cars for such events as Paris–Vienna, Paris–Madrid and the Gordon Bennett races. The car illustrated was the largest of the racing cars, and had a 4-cylinder in-line engine mounted transversely. Nicknamed *Beetle* because of its long bonnet, it finished 12th in the Gordon Bennett, driven by Charles Jarrott (seen here at the wheel). One of these cars came 8th in the 1905 Gordon Bennett, but this was the last year of the Wolseley racing cars, and in 1906 Austin left to set up his own company.

Engine: 4-cyl, 152.4×165.1 mm, 11,896 cc. Coil and battery, overhead valves, 96 bhp.

Transmission: 4-speed, chain drive. 65 mph.

Chassis: Channel-steel, rear brakes. 9 ft wheelbase.

1904 Dufaux
70/90 hp racing car

The Dufaux was the only Swiss-built racing car to contest either the Gordon Bennett races or the early Grand Prix, and was unusual in having a straight-8 engine. The Dufaux brothers had only limited resources and only entered one car in each race. Their 1904 and 1905 entries never reached the starting line, but the 1907 Grand Prix car, which was similar in design, did complete seven of the ten laps of the Grand Prix circuit. The car illustrated can be seen in the Swiss Transport Museum at Lucerne.

Engine: 8-cyl, 125×130 mm, 12,761 cc. High-tension magneto, side valves, 90 bhp.
Transmission: 4-speed, chain drive. 90 mph.
Chassis: Channel-steel, rear brakes. 8 ft 3½ in wheelbase.

1905 White
racing car

The White was one of the best-known American steam cars, and for a short time the makers entered competitions. The car illustrated was built for the 1905 Vanderbilt Cup, and was in fact the only steam car to enter for these races. It retired on the 5th lap, but restarted, and was still running when the race was stopped as the crowd was swarming on to the track. White did not build any more racing cars, although they continued to make steam touring cars until 1911, gasoline touring cars until 1918, and are still well-known truck makers today.

Engine: 2-cyl, 40 bhp.
Transmission: 2-speed, shaft drive. 70 mph.
Chassis: Channel-steel, rear brakes. 9 ft 3 in wheelbase.

1906 Renault
90 hp Grand Prix racing car

By 1906 Renault had adopted their familiar radiator mounted behind the engine which they were to retain until 1929. The three 90 hp cars entered for the first Grand Prix de l'Automobile Club de France, were advanced machines with shaft drive and detachable rims. Renault were among the three makes (out of twelve) in the race to use the latter feature, which made tyre changing much easier and undoubtedly contributed to their victory. The driver was the Hungarian, Ferenc Szisz, seen here at the wheel.

Engine: 4-cyl, 166×150 mm, 12,975 cc. High-tension magneto, side valves, 105 bhp.
Transmission: 3-speed, shaft drive. 100 mph.
Chassis: Channel-steel, rear brakes. 9 ft 6½ in wheelbase.
Events Won: 1906 French Grand Prix.

1906 Locomobile
90 hp racing car

Locomobile were among America's most prestigious car makers in the early days. Their products followed Mercedes' ideas with T-head engines, honeycomb radiators and double chain drive. They built a 17½-litre T-head racing car for the 1905 Gordon Bennett, which did not do well in this event but came 3rd in the Long Island Vanderbilt Cup later that year. Locomobile built another racing car for the 1906 Vanderbilt, this time with inlet-over-exhaust valves and a slightly smaller engine of 16 litres. It had tyre trouble during the race and finished only 10th, but in 1908 it won the Vanderbilt, the first time that an American car had won a major race against European competition.

Engine: 4-cyl, 184.1×158.7 mm, 16,000 cc. Low-tension magneto, inlet over exhaust, 90 bhp.
Transmission: 3-speed, chain drive. 95 mph.
Chassis: Channel-steel, rear brakes.
Events Won: 1908 Vanderbilt Cup.

1907 Christie
Grand Prix racing car

Walter Christie was an independent-minded designer who broke most of the conventions of his day, although in two respects his ideas are current on cars of the 1970s. These are front-wheel drive and transverse mounting of the engine, features of all Christie cars. He also dispensed with any kind of transmission; the wheels were driven directly from the ends of the crankshaft, which took the place of a front axle. 1907 was the only year in which Christie entered the Grand Prix, and he retired on the 5th lap.
Engine: 4-cyl, 185×185 mm, 19,891 cc. Coil and battery.
Transmission: 2-speed, direct to front-wheel drive.
Chassis: Channel-steel. 255 cm wheelbase.

1907 Fiat
Grand Prix racing car

Like Locomobile and other manufacturers on both sides of the Atlantic, the famous Italian house of Fiat drew heavily on Mercedes for their designs. The 1907 Grand Prix cars were developments of their first large racers, the 10½-litre 1904 Gordon Bennett machines, but capacity was up to 15¼ litres and they had all-overhead valves in place of the inlet-over-exhaust system of the earlier cars. They dominated the Grand Prix, the cars of Wagner and Lancia leading at various stages and when they fell out, Nazzaro took over and won.
Engine: 4-cyl, 180×150 mm, 15,268 cc. Low-tension magneto, overhead valves, 130 bhp.
Transmission: 4-speed, chain drive. 98 mph.
Chassis: Channel-steel, rear brakes. 290 cm wheelbase.
Events Won: 1907 French Grand Prix, 1907 Targa Florio.

1908 Itala
Grand Prix racing car

Itala was a leading Italian manufacturer in the early days whose cars were generally similar to Fiats except that they used shaft drive even on their largest models. They built cars for the 1906 and 1908 Grands Prix; all three 1906 entrants either retired or crashed, but in 1908 one of the three team cars finished 11th. The driver was Alessandro Cagno who was also chauffeur to the Queen of Italy.

Engine: 4-cyl, 155×160 mm, 12,060 cc. Low-tension magneto, inlet over exhaust, 115 bhp.
Transmission: 4-speed, shaft drive. 100 mph.
Chassis: Channel-steel, rear brakes. 9 ft 11 in wheelbase.
Events Won: 1910 All-Comers Plate, Brooklands.

1908 Austin
Grand Prix racing car

The Grand Prix Austin was a surprising venture for a company which never went in for major racing events before or since, although the Austin Seven did well in small car competitions. Three cars were built for the 1908 Grand Prix, two with chain drive and one driven by shaft, all using 9.6-litre T-head 6-cylinder engines. They did not have a very high performance, and J. T. C. Moore-Brabazon, one of the drivers, said that they were really fast tourers rather than racing cars. His shaft-driven car finished 18th, and Dario Resta's chain-drive model was 19th. The other Austin retired. The photograph shows Moore-Brabazon at the wheel before the start.

Engine: 6-cyl, 127×127 mm, 9,635 cc. High-tension magneto, side valves, 100 bhp.
Transmission: 4-speed, shaft drive. 96 mph.
Chassis: Channel-steel, rear brakes. 275 cm wheelbase.

1908 Thomas
Grand Prix racing car

The Thomas company earned undying fame in 1908 when one of their 72 hp 6-cylinder touring cars won the gruelling New York to Paris race, covering 12,116 miles in 170 days. Their Grand Prix car had a larger engine and only four cylinders, but like the Austin it was not up to its Continental competition, and the driver Lewis Strang was forced to retire on the 5th lap with clutch trouble.
Engine: 4-cyl, 150×150 mm, 11,321 cc. High-tension magneto, side valves, 60 bhp.
Transmission: 4-speed, chain drive. 95 mph.
Chassis: Channel-steel, rear brakes.

1908 Horch
Prince Henry sports car

The car illustrated can claim to be the
world's first sports car as it was built
intentionally as a high-speed car for
road use, in this case, the 1908 Prince
Henry Trial. The body seated four,
though not in any comfort, and was
intended to minimize wind resistance.
Because of this, the engine was smaller
than many other Prince Henry cars. The
Horches did not distinguish themselves
in the Trial.
Engine: 4-cyl, 85×120 mm, 2,725 cc.
Low-tension magneto, side valves,
25 bhp.
Transmission: 4-speed, shaft drive.
64 mph.
Chassis: Channel steel, rear brakes.
293 cm wheelbase.

1910 Austro-Daimler

sports car

The Austro-Daimlers built for the 1910 Prince Henry Trials were the first significant designs to come from the drawing board of the great Ferdinand Porsche, later responsible for the Targa Florio Mercedes, S series Mercedes-Benz and Auto Union as well as the Volkswagen. The Prince Henry cars were reliable as well as fast, and took first three places in the trials, the winning car being driven by Porsche himself. They were the only chain-driven cars in the event, and continued to use this outmoded transmission system until 1912.

Engine: 4-cyl, 105×165 mm, 5,714 cc. High-tension magneto, overhead valves operated by single ohc, 95 bhp.
Transmission: 4-speed, chain drive. 92 mph.
Chassis: Channel-steel, rear brakes. 3,055 mm wheelbase.
Events Won: 1910 Prince Henry Trial.

1910 Benz

Prince Henry sports tourer

A Benz driven by Fritz Erle won the 1908 Prince Henry Trial without the benefit of streamlining, but for 1910 the company entered a team of the cars illustrated, with cowled radiator top and very clean body lines. The 7.3-litre engine with four overhead valves per cylinder gave the car a speed of nearly 86 mph, faster than that of the Austro-Daimlers, but the best position that Benz could achieve in 1910 was 5th, again with Fritz Erle at the wheel.

Engine: 4-cyl, 115×175 mm, 7,272 cc. High-tension magneto, overhead valves, 115 bhp.
Transmission: 4-speed, shaft drive. 92 mph.
Chassis: Channel-steel, rear brakes. 300 cm wheelbase.

1910   Lion-Peugeot
racing car

The regulations for the Coupe des Voiturettes restricted cylinder bore, but said nothing about the stroke, with the result that some firms built freakish engines whose stroke was anything up to three times the bore. The Lion-Peugeot VX-5 was the most extreme of these, with a bonnet so high that the driver had to peer round rather than look over it. Nevertheless, the car won a number of races and hill climbs, and took records at Brooklands, where it is seen in this photograph.
Engine: 2-cyl, 80×280 mm, 2,816 cc. High-tension magneto, inlet over exhaust (valves).
Transmission: 4-speed, chain drive. 95 mph.
Chassis: Channel-steel, rear brakes.
Events Won: 1910 Sicilian Cup, 1910 Catalan Cup.

1911   Marmon
racing car

The Marmon company of Indianapolis were one of the town's native makes who naturally took to racing at the new Speedway when it was opened in 1909. The first 500 Mile Race took place in 1911, and was won by the 6-cylinder Marmon illustrated, driven by Ray Harroun. It was one of the first single-seater racing cars, and to overcome the objection that the lack of a riding mechanic meant that the driver had no one to warn him of cars approaching from behind, the Marmon carried a rear-view mirror, the first to be fitted to a car.
Engine: 6-cyl, 114.3×127 mm, 7,820 cc. High-tension magneto, side valve in T-head.
Transmission: 3-speed, shaft drive. 85 mph.
Chassis: Channel-steel, rear brakes. 9 ft 8 in wheelbase.
Events Won: 1911 Indianapolis 500 Mile Race.

Ray Harroun
Indianapolis Motor Speedway 1911
Winner

1911 Bugatti
Type 13 racing car

The Type 13 was the first Ettore Bugatti design to be produced in his own factory, previous type numbers referring to cars designed by Bugatti for other companies. It was a well-designed little car with a monobloc 4-cylinder engine with single overhead camshaft, and made its first sporting appearance in the 1911 Monte Carlo Rally. In the Grand Prix de France held in July that year, a Type 13 driven by Ernst Friderich came 2nd, ahead of many machines much larger than itself. The illustration is of this car at the start of the race.

Engine: 4-cyl, 66×100 mm, 1,368 cc. High-tension magneto, overhead valves operated by single ohc.
Transmission: 4-speed, shaft drive.
Chassis: Channel-steel, rear brakes. 7 ft 7 in wheelbase.

1912 Lorraine-Dietrich
Grand Prix racing car

The Grand Prix of 1912 saw the end of an era in motor racing, for cars which relied on sheer size of engine for their power were convincingly beaten by a smaller car whose engine made up in design what it lacked in litres, the 7.6-litre Peugeot. This Lorraine-Dietrich was the last of the 'dinosaurs', with a capacity of over 15 litres. None of the four cars in the team finished the race, and the result so discouraged the makers that they never entered Grand Prix racing again. They did, however, build some successful sports cars in the 1920s. The front mudguards, as on a touring car, were distinctly unusual in Grand Prix racing.
Engine: 4-cyl, 155×200 mm, 15,095 cc. Dual high-tension magnetos, overhead valves.
Transmission: 4-speed, chain drive.
Chassis: Channel-steel, rear brakes.

1912 Sizaire-Naudin
racing car

From 1906 to 1909 the French firm of Sizaire-Naudin built long-stroke single-cylinder racing voiturettes which had many successes in events such as the Coupe des Voiturettes and Sicilian Cup. For the 1912 Coupe de l'Auto they built three 4-cylinder cars with four horizontal valves per cylinder. They were supposed to have superchargers, but none were seen on the cars when they came to the start of the race. In fact, they were seriously underpowered, and none completed the course. They were successful in hill climbs, however.

Engine: 4-cyl, 78×156 mm, 2,962 cc. High-tension magneto, side valves in T-head.

Transmission: 4-speed, shaft drive. 95 mph.

Chassis: Channel-steel, rear brakes.

1913 Bédélia
racing cyclecar

The cyclecar was a new type of motorcar which appeared in about 1910, lighter and simpler in construction than normal cars, and owing a lot to motorcycle practice. Two Cyclecar Grands Prix were held in France in 1913, at Amiens and at Le Mans. The former event was won by a Bédélia similar to the one illustrated. Like its touring counterparts, it was a most unusual car, with the driver in the rear seat and the front 'passenger' responsible for changing gear.
Engine: 2-cyl, 82×100 mm, 1,056 cc. High-tension magneto, inlet over exhaust (valves).
Transmission: 2-speed, belt drive. 60 mph.
Chassis: Wooden punt, rear brakes. 8 ft $4\frac{3}{4}$ in wheelbase.
Events Won: 1913 Amiens Cyclecar Grand Prix.

1913 Delage
Grand Prix racing car

Although the Delage company had built a number of successful small racing cars, they did not venture into the Grand Prix field until 1913, when they entered a team of two cars with 4-cylinder engines, four horizontal valves per cylinder and five-speed gearboxes. Albert Guyot's car led for six laps and seemed all set to win when a tyre burst, his mechanic jumped out too soon and was run over by the rear wheel. Guyot drove the injured man to the pits, and then resumed the race, but he had lost fifteen minutes and finished no higher than fifth. Another Delage was fourth. In 1914 one of these cars won the Indianapolis 500 Mile Race in America.

Engine: 4-cyl, 110×185 mm, 7,032 cc. High-tension magneto, horizontal overhead valves, 105 bhp.
Transmission: 5-speed, shaft drive. 100 mph.
Chassis: Channel-steel, rear brakes.
Events Won: 1913 Grand Prix de France (a different race from the above). 1914 Indianapolis 500 Mile Race.

1913 Hispano-Suiza
Alfonso sports car

One of the first vehicles deserving the title of sports car, the Alfonso was named after the king of Spain who had taken delivery of his first Hispano-Suiza car in 1905. His first Alfonso was a present from his wife in 1910, and he later owned several others. Its long-stroke engine was derived from the company's successful racing voiturettes, and gave them an effortless and unstrained top-gear performance, with a maximum speed of over 80 mph with the highest of the two alternative rear-axle ratios. The Alfonso was made from 1911 to 1914 at two factories, Barcelona and Levallois-Perret.

Engine: 4-cyl, 80×180 mm, 3,620 cc. High-tension magneto, side valves in T-head, 64 bhp.
Transmission: 3- or 4-speed, shaft drive. 77 mph.
Chassis: Channel-steel, rear brakes. 8 ft 8 in or 9 ft 10 in wheelbase.

1914 Vauxhall
Prince Henry tourer

Like the Austro-Daimler, the Vauxhall was another excellent sporting car to result from the 1910 Prince Henry Trials. The first cars sold to the public, in 1911, had 3-litre engines and four seater tourer bodies with no doors, but a modified version carried small doors as in the car illustrated. This also has the larger engine introduced in 1913. The following year a still larger engine of $4\frac{1}{2}$ litres was built, the resulting car being known as the 30/98.

Engine: 4-cyl, 95×140 mm, 3,971 cc. High-tension magneto, side valves, 75 bhp.

Transmission: 4-speed, shaft drive. 85 mph.

Chassis: Channel-steel, rear brakes. 9 ft 6 in wheelbase.

1914 Duesenberg

racing car

The first racing cars designed by Fred Duesenberg were built in the works of the Mason Automobile Company, for whom Duesenberg worked, and were raced under the name Mason in 1912. Two years later the Duesenberg brothers set up their own works in St Paul, Minnesota where cars like the one illustrated were made. Their 4-cylinder engines had two horizontal valves per cylinder, operated by large, vertical rocker arms from which was derived the name 'walking-beam engine'. These cars were raced by well-known drivers like Eddie Rickenbacker, Tommy Milton and Ralph Mulford, and were made up to the end of American pre-war racing in 1916.
Engine: 4-cyl, 111×152 mm, 5,920 cc. High-tension magneto, horizontal overhead valves, 100 bhp.
Transmission: 4-speed, shaft drive. 105 mph.
Chassis: Channel-steel, rear brakes. 8 ft 10 in wheelbase.
Events Won: 1914 Sioux City 300 Mile Race, 1915 Des Moines Board Track 300 Mile Race, 1916 Corona 300 Mile Race, 1916 Ascot 150 Mile Race.

1914 Mercedes
Grand Prix racing car

After several years of absence, Mercedes made a modest comeback in 1913 and a much more dramatic one next year. They brought five cars, and although their design was not the most modern (they did not have front-wheel brakes), their preparation and team work was magnificent, and a foretaste of the Mercedes-Benz racing organization of the 1930s. They tested six alternative final drive ratios during practice, and in the race Sailer deliberately drove as fast as possible to break up the Peugeot opposition, not caring that he retired on the sixth lap as there were still four of his team-mates in the race. The final result was a 1-2-3 victory for Mercedes.

Engine: 4-cyl, 93×165 mm, 4,483 cc. Dual high-tension magneto, overhead valves operated by single ohc, 115 bhp.
Transmission: 4-speed, shaft drive. 115 mph.
Chassis: Channel-steel, rear brakes. 9 ft 4 in wheelbase.
Events Won: 1914 French Grand Prix, 1914 Chicago Cup, 1914 Elgin Trophy, 1915 Indianapolis 500 Mile Race, 1922 Targa Florio.

1914 Peugeot
Grand Prix racing car

In 1912 a Peugeot ushered in a new era of motor racing when a 7.6-litre car with modern twin overhead camshaft engine defeated much larger cars with old-fashioned pushrod engines. The 1914 car illustrated continued the twin-ohc theme, but in accordance with the Grand Prix formula, had a smaller engine of $4\frac{1}{2}$ litres. Nevertheless, specific output was greater at 24 bhp per litre compared with 17.1 bhp per litre from the 1912 car. It was also the first GP Peugeot to have front-wheel brakes. In the race, George Boillot led for most of the time, but was eventually overtaken by the Mercedes, and retired shortly before the finish.

Engine: 4-cyl, 92×169 mm, 4,400 cc. High-tension magneto, overhead valves operated by twin ohc, 112 bhp.

Transmission: 4-speed, shaft drive. 112 mph.

Chassis: Channel-steel, 4-wheel brakes.

Events Won: 1915 Vanderbilt Cup, 1915 Cincinnati 300 Mile Race, 1915 Sheepshead Bay 100 Mile Race, 1916 and 1919 Indianapolis 500 Mile Race, 1916 Chicago 300 Mile Race, 1916 Grand Prize.

1915 Stutz
racing car

The Stutz company from Indianapolis made its name with the Bearcat roadster, one of America's first sports cars. It had a T-head engine which was also used by the first Stutz racing cars, but in 1915 the company ordered a specially designed racing engine with single overhead camshaft and four valves per cylinder. Three cars were built using these engines, and were known as the White Squadron. With drivers Eddie Hearne, Earl Cooper and Gil Anderson they won the American Automobile Association National Championship for 1915.

Engine: 4-cyl, 97×165 mm, 4,916 cc. High-tension magneto, overhead valves operated by single ohc, 130 bhp.

Transmission: 3-speed, shaft drive. 100 mph.

Chassis: Channel-steel, rear brakes. 8 ft 8 in wheelbase.

Events Won: 1915 Point Loma Road Race, 1915 Minneapolis 500 Mile Race, 1915 Elgin Road Race, 1915 Sheepshead Bay 350 Mile Race, 1917 Chicago Board Track 250 Mile Race.

1919 Ballot
racing car

The Ballot company sprang on to the motor racing scene without warning in 1919, for their previous products had been proprietary engines with no sporting characteristics. Ernest Ballot engaged the Swiss designer Ernest Henry (who had been responsible for the Grand Prix Peugeots) and in 101 days a brand new racing car was designed and built, being ready for the Indianapolis 500 Mile Race at the end of May 1919. Like the 1914 Peugeot, the Ballot had twin overhead camshafts operating inclined overhead valves, but it had eight cylinders, being the first straight-8 car to achieve any success in motor racing. The four cars that ran at Indianapolis were overgeared, and their best place was Albert Guyot's 4th. They later did well in hill climbs.

Engine: 8-cyl, 74 × 140 mm, 4,820 cc. High-tension magneto, overhead valves operated by twin ohc, 140 bhp.
Transmission: 4-speed, shaft drive. 118 mph.
Chassis: Channel-steel, rear brakes. 8 ft 8½ in wheelbase.
Records: 1919 Gaillon Hill Climb.

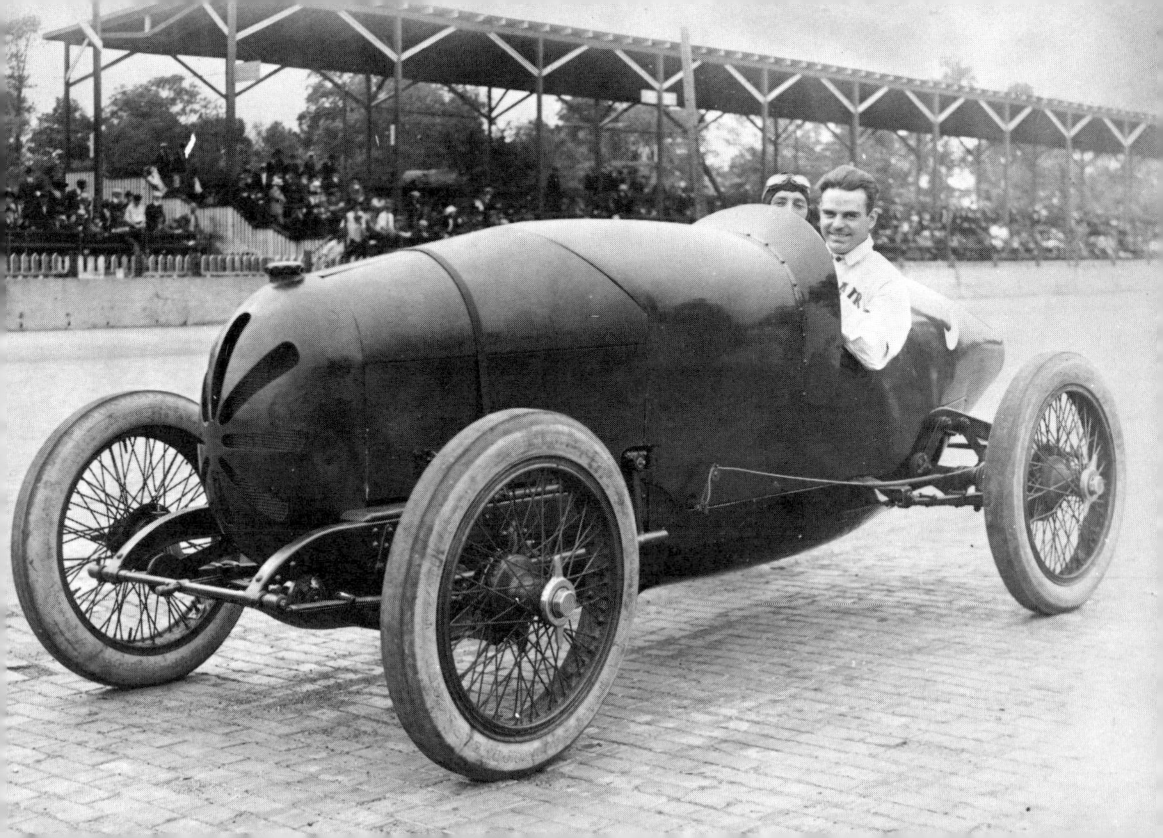

1920 Frontenac
racing car

Frontenac cars were designed by Louis Chevrolet who gave his name to what was to become America's best-selling car. The first Frontenacs appeared in 1916, and this 1920 model was the first post-war design, and the most successful. It had a twin-ohc engine, and was built in the factory of the Monroe company of Indianapolis. No fewer than seven cars were entered for Indianapolis, and although five retired, Gaston Chevrolet, Louis' brother, won at a speed of 88.17 mph. 1921 Frontenacs had 8-cylinder engines, but were not so successful as the 4-cylinder cars.

Engine: 4-cyl, 79×152 mm, 2,980 cc. Coil, overhead valves operated by twin ohc, 98 bhp.
Transmission: 3-speed, shaft drive. 100 mph.
Chassis: Channel-steel, rear brakes. 8 ft 2 in wheelbase.
Events Won: 1920 Indianapolis 500 Mile Race.

1921 Duesenberg
racing car

In 1919 the Duesenberg company built a straight-8 engine with single overhead camshaft, abandoning the 'walking-beam' layout of their original engines. The 1919 car, of 4.9-litres capacity, was not particularly successful, and the following year they built a smaller engine of 3 litres to comply with the prevailing regulations for Indianapolis. This made the car also eligible for Grand Prix racing in Europe, and four cars, now equipped with hydraulic four-wheel brakes, were entered for the 1921 French Grand Prix. Jimmy Murphy (at the wheel in the photo) won, to become the first American driver to win a European Grand Prix, and in an American car too.

Engine: 8-cyl, 63.5×117 mm, 2,980 cc. Coil, overhead valves operated by single ohc, 115 bhp.
Transmission: 3-speed, shaft drive. 114 mph.
Chassis: Channel-steel, 4-wheel brakes. 8 ft 4 in wheelbase.
Events Won: 1921 French Grand Prix, 1921 Cotati Board Track Race, 1921 Beverly Hills Board Track Race.

1921 Chitty-Bang-Bang

racing car

The name Chitty-Bang-Bang is today associated with the magic car of Ian Fleming's story and film, but to racegoers of the early 'twenties it was a very real motorcar, three of them in fact bearing the name. They were designed and built by Count Louis Zborowski with the aim of providing really powerful cars for road and track use, at not too great expense. Thus the engines came from the Aircraft Disposal Company, and had first seen service in aeroplanes or airships. The car illustrated, Chitty 1, had a 23-litre Maybach engine. Next to Chitty is a 2-cylinder racing GN 'Mowgli', whose engine capacity was little more than $\frac{1}{20}$th that of the big car's.

Engine: 6-cyl, 165×180 mm, 23,092 cc. High-tension magneto, overhead valves, 305 bhp.
Transmission: 4-speed, chain drive. 125 mph.
Chassis: Channel-steel, rear brakes.
Events Won: 1921 100 mph Short Handicap, Brooklands, 1921 Lightning Short Handicap, Brooklands.

1914 Bugatti
racing car

The first post-war Bugatti cars were a continuation of the pre-war theme of small high-quality machines, but with slightly enlarged engines with four valves per cylinder. The latter feature had been used on the cars built for the 1914 Coupe des Voiturettes which had never taken place, and the car illustrated is one of these, seen before the start of the 1920 Coupe des Voiturettes at Le Mans. Driven by Ernst Friderich, it won the race. Post-war cars took the first four places in the 1921 Voiturette Grand Prix at Brescia in Italy, and this led to the name Brescia being applied to all the small post-war Bugattis.

Engine: 4-cyl, 66×100 mm, 1,368 cc. High-tension magneto, overhead valves operated by single ohc, 40 bhp.
Transmission: 4-speed, shaft drive.
Chassis: Channel-steel, rear brakes. 7 ft 7 in wheelbase.
Events Won: 1920 Le Mans Coupe de Voiturettes.

1922 Bignan

sports car

Like Ballot, Bignan was a company which had built proprietary engines before going in for complete cars. A 3-litre ohc-engined car won the 1921 Corsican Grand Prix (a sports car event), and for 1922 Bignan's chief engineer, Causan, designed a 2-litre engine with desmodromic valves, which were closed positively instead of by a spring in the usual way. This was supposed to provide quicker action, but the cars so equipped did not do particularly well. The photo shows one of the desmodromic cars during the 1922 Touring Car Grand Prix at Strasbourg.

Engine: 4-cyl, 75 × 112 mm, 1,980 cc. High-tension magneto, overhead desmodromic valves, 70 bhp.
Transmission: 4-speed, shaft drive. 100 mph.
Chassis: Channel-steel, 4-wheel brakes.
Events Won: 1922 Belgian Grand Prix (2-litre class), 1924 Belgian Grand Prix.
Records: 1924 World 24 Hour.

1921 Hispano-Suiza
sports car

The Alfonso Hispano was not re-introduced after the war, and instead the French factory launched a very up-to-date, luxurious car powered by a 6-cylinder single-ohc engine, using servo-operated four-wheel brakes. It was primarily intended as a touring chassis for open or closed bodies, but it had obvious attractions for the sportsman, including the aperitif millionaire André Dubonnet. He entered his standard car (illustrated) in the 1921 Georges Boillot Cup at Boulogne, and won the event. This led to Hispano building a team of cars with larger engines for the next year's Boillot Cup, which they also won. The large-engined, short-chassis cars came to be known as the Boulogne models.

Engine: 6-cyl, 100×140 mm, 6,600 cc. High-tension magneto, overhead valves operated by single ohc, 134 bhp.

Transmission: 3-speed, shaft drive. 85 mph.

Chassis: Channel-steel, 4-wheel servo-operated brakes. 12 ft 1½ in wheelbase.

Events Won: 1921 Coupe Boillot.

1922 Fiat
Grand Prix racing car

Fiat supported Grand Prix racing actively from 1921 to 1927, and for the 1922 2-litre Formula they built a team of 6-cylinder cars similar in design to their 1921 straight-8s. Three cars ran in the French Grand Prix at Strasbourg, that of Felice Nazzaro winning at 79.20 mph. The other two cars both fell out with broken rear axles, a simple retirement in the case of Pietro Bordino and a fatal crash for Biagio Nazzaro, nephew of Felice.
Engine: 6-cyl, 65×100 mm, 1,995 cc. High-tension magneto, overhead valves operated by twin ohc, 92 bhp.
Transmission: 4-speed, shaft drive. 105 mph.
Chassis: Channel-steel, 4-wheel brakes. 8 ft 2½ in wheelbase.
Events Won: 1922 French Grand Prix, 1922 Italian Grand Prix.

1923 Sunbeam
Grand Prix racing car

The 1923 Sunbeam GP cars were designed by Vincent Bertarione who was Fiat's designer until 1922, and they were very like the 1922 Fiat GP cars. In the 1923 French Grand Prix, a Sunbeam driven by H. O. D. Segrave won at a speed of 75.3 mph, while his team-mates Albert Divo and K. L. Guinness (in the photo) came 2nd and 4th respectively. This was the first time that a British car and driver had won a Grand Prix.
Engine: 6-cyl, 67×94 mm, 1,988 cc. High-tension magneto, overhead valves operated by twin ohc, 102 bhp.
Transmission: 3-speed, shaft drive. 100 mph.
Chassis: Channel-steel, 4-wheel brakes. 8 ft 2 in wheelbase.
Events Won: 1923 French Grand Prix.

1923 Benz
Grand Prix racing car

In 1923 the company engaged Edmund Rumpler who was a pioneer designer of rear-engined cars, and he designed for them the radical *Tropfenwagen* (teardrop car) illustrated. It had a 6-cylinder engine behind the driver but ahead of the rear axle, making it a mid-engined car. Rear suspension was independent by swing axles, and another advanced feature was the inboard mounting of the rear brakes. They competed in one major race, the 1923 European Grand Prix, when they finished 4th and 5th.
Engine: 6-cyl, 65×100 mm, 1,995 cc. High-tension magneto, overhead valves operated by twin ohc, 80 bhp.
Transmission: 4-speed, shaft drive. 110 mph.
Chassis: Channel-steel, 4-wheel brakes. 9 ft 1½ in wheelbase.

1924 Alfa Romeo
Grand Prix car

Alfa Romeo built their first Grand Prix cars in 1914, but they did not race as they were not ready in time, and they did not enter GP racing again until 1924. This was with the P2, a new design by Vittorio Jano who had come to Alfa from Fiat, and it won the very first race it was entered in, the Circuit of Cremona. Much more important was Giuseppe Campari's victory in the French Grand Prix at Tours, against very strong opposition from Bugatti, Delage, Fiat and Sunbeam teams.

Engine: 8-cyl, 61×85 mm, 1,987 cc. High-tension magneto, overhead valves operated by twin ohc, 165 bhp.
Transmission: 4-speed, shaft drive. 135 mph.
Chassis: Channel-steel, 4-wheel brakes. 8 ft 6 in wheelbase.
Events Won: 1924 Circuit of Cremona, 1924 French Grand Prix, 1925 Belgian Grand Prix, 1925 Italian Grand Prix, 1927 and 1928 Coppa Acerbo.

1924 Vauxhall
30/98 sports car

The Vauxhall 30/98 was introduced before World War I, but very few were made. Re-introduced in 1919 it rapidly became one of the most desirable fast touring cars on the market, although it was never raced to the extent of its rival the Bentley. In 1922 the side-valve E-type was replaced by the OE with overhead valves and a slightly smaller capacity of 4,224 cc (illustrated).

Engine: 4-cyl, 98×140 mm, 4,224 cc. High-tension magneto, side valves, 112 bhp.

Transmission: 4-speed, shaft drive. 85 mph.

Chassis: Channel-steel, 4-wheel brakes. 9 ft 9 in wheelbase.

1921 Bentley
3-litre sports car

The 3-litre Bentley was one of the first British sports cars to be announced after World War I, the initial notice appearing in May 1919, but production difficulties prevented any cars coming into private hands until more than two years later. More than any other car, the 3-litre has come to be regarded as the epitome of the British vintage sports car, and it was well on its way to acquiring this reputation during its lifetime, thanks to victory at Le Mans in 1924 and its choice by novelists such as Sapper for their heroes to drive. The car illustrated is one of the oldest surviving examples of the 3-litre, and is fitted with Number One engine.

Engine: 4-cyl, 80×149 mm, 2,996 cc. High-tension magneto, overhead valves operated by single ohc.
Transmission: 4-speed, shaft drive. 75 mph.
Chassis: Channel-steel, 4-wheel brakes. 9 ft 9½ in wheelbase.
Events Won: 1924 Le Mans 24 Hour Race.

1923   Chenard-Walcker
3-litre tourer

The Chenard-Walcker is best known as the winner of the first of the 24 Hour Touring Car Races at Le Mans, held in 1923. These 3-litre cars were unusual in that they had Hallot servo brakes on the front wheels, while rear-wheel braking was by a transmission brake, there being no drums on the rear wheels themselves. In 1924 the 3-litre was joined by a new 4-litre straight-8 car which led the race at Le Mans for 20 hours before retiring. In 1925 the 4-litre was given conventional four-wheel brakes, and won the Belgian 24 Hour Race at Spa.

Engine: 4-cyl, 79.5×150 mm, 2,979 cc. High-tension magneto, overhead valves operated by single ohc.
Transmission: 4-speed, shaft drive. 75 mph.
Chassis: Channel-steel, front and transmission brakes. 10 ft 2 in wheelbase.
Events Won: 1923 Le Mans 24 Hour Race, 1924 Circuit des Routes Pavées.

1924 Bugatti
Type 35 Grand Prix racing car

The Type 35 Bugatti was probably the most successful racing car ever made, winning countless events between 1924 and 1930. In its original form it had a 2-litre straight-8 engine, but smaller engines of 1.5 and even 1.1 litres were made to suit the 1925 and 1926 Grands Prix formula. Superchargers were fitted to most models from 1925 onwards and in 1926, the engine was enlarged to 2.3 litres in the Type 35B. The Type 35A was similar in appearance to the other models, but had a touring engine and was considerably cheaper. The photograph shows the prototype Type 35 at Lyons in 1924 with Ettore Bugatti at the wheel and the Préfet du Rhone at his side.

Engine: 8-cyl, 60×88 mm, 1,990 cc. High-tension magneto, overhead valves operated by single ohc, 105 bhp.
Transmission: 4-speed, shaft drive. 110 mph.
Chassis: Channel-steel, 4-wheel brakes. 7 ft 10½ in wheelbase.
Events Won: 1925 Rome Grand Prix, 1926 French Grand Prix, 1926 European Grand Prix, 1926 Spanish Grand Prix, 1926 Italian Grand Prix.

1924 Mercedes

Targa Florio racing car

The Mercedes company entered regularly in the great Sicilian race, the Targa Florio, from 1921 to 1924, winning in 1922 and 1924. For the latter event they built four cars with 4-cylinder 2-litre engines similar to the cars they ran at Indianapolis in 1923.

Engine: 4-cyl, 70×129 mm, 1,990 cc. High-tension magneto, overhead valves operated by twin ohc, 120 bhp.
Transmission: 4-speed, shaft drive. 115 mph.
Chassis: Channel-steel, 4-wheel brakes. 8 ft 7 in wheelbase.
Events Won: 1924 Targa Florio, 1924 Solitude Race.

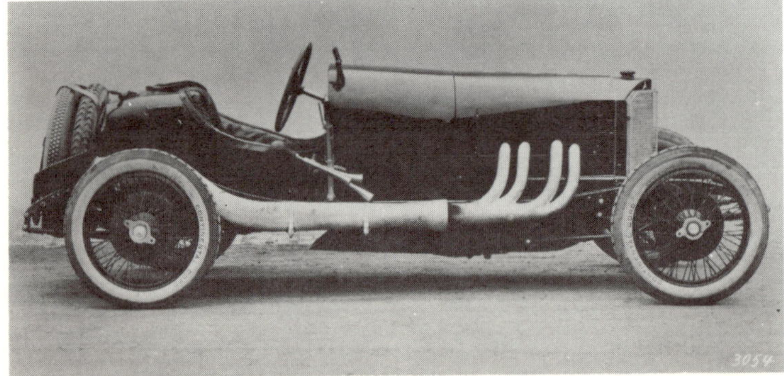

1926 Lorraine-Dietrich
$3\frac{1}{2}$-litre sports car

The $3\frac{1}{2}$-litre, or 15CV as it was known in France, Lorraine-Dietrich was derived from a relatively cheap touring car designed by Marius Barbarou in 1919. In 1924 a sports model was offered, with front-wheel brakes, larger valves, twin carburettors and dual ignition. These cars won at Le Mans in 1925 and 1926 and were still competing there in 1935 when they were real oldsters. The car in the photograph is preparing to start in the 1927 Touring Car Grand Prix at Guipuzcoa in Spain.

Engine: 6-cyl, 75×130 mm, 3,445 cc. High-tension magneto, overhead valves.
Transmission: 4-speed, shaft drive. 88 mph.
Chassis: Channel-steel, 4-wheel brakes. 10 ft 3 in wheelbase.
Events Won: 1925 and 1926 Le Mans 24 Hour Race.

1925 Delage
Grand Prix racing car

In 1923 Delage built the first 12-cylinder car to compete in a Grand Prix, and although it made only one appearance that year and failed to finish, it was the forerunner of a series of V-12 2-litre cars which culminated in the 1925 car illustrated. This had a supercharged engine and a very high performance for which the roadholding and brakes were hardly adequate. Nevertheless they came 1st and 2nd in the French Grand Prix, and 1st, 2nd and 3rd in the Spanish Grand Prix.

Engine: 12-cyl, 51.3×80 mm, 1,995 cc. High-tension magneto, overhead valves operated by 4 ohc, 195 bhp.
Transmission: 4-speed, shaft drive. 135 mph.
Chassis: Channel-steel, 4-wheel brakes. 8 ft 6 in wheelbase.
Events Won: 1925 French Grand Prix, 1925 San Sebastian Grand Prix.

1925 Miller
racing car

From 1922 to 1929 Miller cars dominated American racing, and Miller engines in other chassis won every Indianapolis 500 Mile Race from 1930 to 1938. In 1925 the front-wheel-drive Miller was introduced, of which the car illustrated was the second to be built. It was raced under the name Junior Eight, being sponsored by the Locomobile car company whose touring car was called the Junior Eight. Dave Lewis and Bennett Hill (in the photo) drove it into 2nd place in the 1925 500 Mile Race.
Engine: 8-cyl, 60×89 mm, 1,980 cc. High-tension magneto, overhead valves operated by twin ohc, 125 bhp.
Transmission: 3-speed, front-wheel drive. 135 mph.
Chassis: Channel-steel, 4-wheel brakes. 8 ft 4 in wheelbase.

1927 Salmson
sports car

France had a large number of small sports car makes in the 1920s, but the two best-known were Salmson and Amilcar. From 1923 onwards all Salmsons had twin overhead camshaft engines, and by 1926 sports models had cowled radiators and front-wheel brakes. Generally Salmsons were cheaper than the equivalent Amilcars, while the most powerful Salmson, the supercharged San Sebastian, was more than a match for any Amilcar.

Engine: 4-cyl, 62.2×90 mm, 1,087 cc. High-tension magneto, overhead valves operated by twin ohc, 36 bhp.
Transmission: 3-speed, shaft drive. 75 mph.
Chassis: Channel-steel, 4-wheel brakes. 8 ft 6 in wheelbase.

1927 Austin
Seven sports car

The popular little Austin Seven was widely used for trials and racing almost from the date of its introduction in 1922. Among the most famous sports models was the Gordon England which was sold with a certificate guaranteeing that it had lapped Brooklands at 75 mph. It cost £265, compared with £175 for the milder factory-built sports model. The car illustrated was taking part in the Surbiton Motor Club's 150 Mile Race at Brooklands in September 1927.

Engine: 4-cyl, 56×76 mm, 747 cc. High-tension magneto, side valves, 25 bhp.
Transmission: 3-speed, shaft drive. 75 mph.
Chassis: Channel-steel, 4-wheel brakes. 6 ft 3 in wheelbase.

1928 Amilcar
CGSS sports car

The first Amilcars, built in 1920, were little two-seater touring cars rather than sports cars, but these followed in 1922 with the CS Petit Sport which had a pointed tail and staggered seating. The later CGS had front-wheel brakes and a more powerful engine, and developed from this was the CGSS which had a lowered chassis and cycle type wings, making it look a much more modern car. This model was made up to 1929, and Amilcars were also built under licence in Germany, Austria and Italy.

Engine: 4-cyl, 60×95 mm, 1,074 cc. High-tension magneto, side valves, 35 bhp.
Transmission: 4-speed, shaft drive. 75—80 mph.
Chassis: Channel-steel, 4-wheel brakes. 7 ft 7 in wheelbase.

1924 Alfa Romeo
RLSS sports car

As well as the P2 Grand Prix cars Alfa Romeo turned out a line of 6-cylinder sports cars during the 1920s known as the RL series. The RLSS was the most sporting of these, and a special model won the 1923 Targa Florio. One of the better-known owners of an RLSS was Benito Mussolini. The photograph shows the French driver Louis Wagner at the wheel of an early RLSS chassis.

Engine: 6-cyl, 76×110 mm, 2,994 cc. High-tension magneto, overhead valves, 83 bhp.

Transmission: 4-speed, shaft drive. 81 mph.

Chassis: Channel-steel, 4-wheel brakes. 10 ft 3 in wheelbase.

1931 Alvis
12/60 sports car

The Alvis 12/50 was one of the best British sports cars of the vintage period, having a useful performance combined with reliability and long life. Developed in 1923 from its predecessor the 11/40, the 12/50 was made until 1932, by which date about 7,000 had been built. The most familiar sporting bodies were the 'duck's back' with pointed tail and the sloping tail 'beetle back', although four-seaters and saloons were also made. The photo shows a duck's back bodied 12/60, which was a higher performance version of the 12/50, but with the same size engine.

Engine: 4-cyl, 68×103 mm, 1,496 cc. High-tension magneto, overhead valves.
Transmission: 4-speed, shaft drive.
Chassis: Channel-steel, 4-wheel brakes. 9 ft ½ in wheelbase.

1926 NSU

1½-litre racing car

The company which today makes the revolutionary Ro80 Wankel-engined car built a number of sports and racing cars in the 1920s. The fastest of these was the 1½-litre 6-cylinder car illustrated which used a Roots-type supercharger driven from the gearbox. Unlike the Mercedes supercharger, which was brought into use by a pedal, the NSU's ran constantly. A team of four of these cars ran in the 1926 German Grand Prix, and finished 1st, 2nd, 3rd and 4th in their class. Financial difficulties prevented the NSU company from continuing their racing programme.

Engine: 6-cyl, 59.1×90 mm, 1,482 cc. High-tension magneto, overhead valves, 60 bhp, Roots-type supercharger.
Transmission: 4-speed, shaft drive. 115 mph.
Chassis: Channel-steel, 4-wheel brakes. 285 cm wheelbase.
Events Won: 1926 German Grand Prix (1½-litre class).

1926 Sunbeam
3-litre sports car

The twin-cam 3-litre Sunbeam's engine was derived from that of the 1923 Bertarione-designed Grand Prix car. The car's first appearance was at Le Mans in 1925 when Jean Chassagne and Sammy Davis drove one into 2nd place, but later production cars never lived up to this early promise. The Sunbeam company was not in good shape, their designer Louis Coatalen was moved to the associated Darracq company in France, and little development work was done on the 3-litre. It was a fine touring car, but with a shorter and stronger chassis it might well have been one of the best sports cars of the 1920s. About 250 were made, production lasting until 1929.

Engine: 6-cyl, 75×110 mm, 2,916 cc. High-tension magneto, overhead valves operated by twin ohc, 95 bhp, Cozette supercharger available on special order.

Transmission: 4-speed, shaft drive. 90 mph.

Chassis: Channel-steel, 4-wheel brakes. 10 ft 10½ in wheelbase.

1929 Chrysler
sports car

Walter Chrysler's 6-cylinder cars always had a higher performance than average for their price, and one competed at Le Mans in 1925, only a year after the make was launched on the market. They raced again at Le Mans in 1928, 1929 and 1931, always with cars very similar to those one could buy in the showroom. The photograph shows the car driven by De Vere and Mangin, which finished 7th in 1929.

Engine: 6-cyl, 82×127 mm, 4,086 cc. High-tension magneto, side valves, 72 bhp.
Transmission: 3-speed, shaft drive.
Chassis: Channel-steel, 4-wheel brakes. 9 ft 1 in wheelbase.

1929   Dupont

sports car

The Dupont was a quality American car built from 1919 to 1932,
of which only one model could be called sporting. This was the
Model G, powered by a 125 bhp straight-8 engine made by
Continental, and usually carrying a two-seater roadster body.
For the 1929 Le Mans race Dupont entered two four-seater
Model Gs, but only one started, and this retired on the 20th
lap, after ballast had fallen through the floor and broken the
propeller shaft.
Engine: 8-cyl, 85.7×114.3 mm, 5,274 cc. High-tension
magneto, side valves, 125 bhp.
Transmission: 3- or 4-speed, shaft drive. 90 mph.
Chassis: Channel-steel, 4-wheel brakes. 11 ft 9 in wheelbase.

1927 Riley
Nine sports car

The Riley Nine touring car appeared in 1926, and was an interesting design with an engine using two camshafts mounted high in the block although not overhead. Riley used this layout until they ceased to make their own engines in 1957. The very low Brooklands Nine sports car was developed by Parry Thomas working at Brooklands track, and after his death while attempting to break the Land Speed Record in March 1927, development was carried on by Reid Railton. The first few Brooklands Nines were assembled at Brooklands, but later models were built by Riley at Coventry. The photo shows the prototype at Brooklands.

Engine: 4-cyl, 60.3×95.2 mm, 1,089 cc. High-tension magneto, overhead valves, 50 bhp.
Transmission: 4-speed, shaft drive. 80 mph.
Chassis: Channel-steel, 4-wheel brakes. 8 ft wheelbase.
Events Won: 1928, 1929, 1930 and 1931 Tourist Trophy (1,100 cc class), 1930 Saorstat Cup, 1932 Tourist Trophy (overall).

1929 Mercedes-Benz
SSK sports car

The legendary Mercedes-Benz sports cars of the late 1920s were derived from a 6.2-litre 6-cylinder car designed by Ferdinand Porsche in 1925, just before the Mercedes firm's merger with Benz. This was the Type K, followed in 1927 by the lower and more powerful Type S, and in 1928 by the SS and short-chassis SSK. The latter was nearly always made in open two-seater form, and racing versions had many successes, particularly when driven by Rudolf Caracciola. The photograph shows Caracciola at the wheel of an SSK before the start of the 1929 Monaco Grand Prix. All the other competitors were full Grand Prix racing cars.

Engine: 6-cyl, 100×150 mm, 7,069 cc. High-tension magneto, overhead valves operated by single ohc, 250 bhp, Mercedes-type supercharger.

Transmission: 4-speed, shaft drive. 120 mph.

Chassis: Channel-steel, 4-wheel brakes. 9 ft 8 in wheelbase.

Events Won: 1930 Irish Grand Prix, 1931 German Grand Prix, 1930 and 1931 European Hill Climb Championship.

1930 MG

M-type Midget sports car

The first MG Midget was developed in 1928 from the single overhead camshaft Morris Minor touring car, and was mechanically similar to the Morris except for lowered suspension and raked steering, and of course the light fabric sports body. It was remarkably good value at £175, and more were sold in the first year of production than all previous MGs. A team of five M-types ran in the 1930 Brooklands Double 12 Hour Race, finishing 3rd, 4th, 5th, 6th and 7th in their class. The photograph shows Miss Victoria Worsley with her Double 12 team car.

Engine: 4-cyl, 57×83 mm, 847 cc. High-tension magneto, overhead valves operated by single ohc, 20 bhp.
Transmission: 3-speed, shaft drive. 65 mph.
Chassis: Channel-steel, 4-wheel brakes. 6 ft 6 in wheelbase.

1932   Invicta
$4\frac{1}{2}$-litre sports car

The low-chassis Invicta was introduced in 1930, using the $4\frac{1}{2}$-litre 6-cylinder Meadows engine of the high-chassis car in an entirely new frame which gave it a much lower appearance than any other large sports car of its day. It has been called the '100 mph' model, although most had a maximum speed of 90 mph, only the last 1934 models being capable of 'the ton'. Although the low-chassis Invicta was raced, it achieved more success in rallies; Donald Healey won the 1931 Monte Carlo in one, and Cups were won in the International Alpine, and Austrian and Hungarian Alpine Trials.

Engine: 6-cyl, 88.5×120 mm, 4,467 cc. High-tension magneto, overhead valves, 120 bhp.
Transmission: 4-speed, shaft drive. 90 mph.
Chassis: Channel-steel, 4-wheel brakes. 9 ft 10 in wheelbase.

1931 Talbot
105 sports car

The 105 was the final development in a line of Talbots which began with the 1.6-litre 14/45 of 1927. Developed by the brilliant designer Georges Roesch, the first sporting model of the series, the 2.3-litre '90', appeared in 1930. These cars finished 3rd and 4th at Le Mans behind much larger and more expensive cars. With a longer wheelbase and engine enlarged to 3 litres, the '90' became the '105' in 1931. This model had many successes at Brooklands, and also won Alpine Cups in the 1931, 1932 and 1934 International Alpine Trials. The four team cars all survive, and are owned by Anthony Blight, a solicitor in Cornwall.

Engine: 6-cyl, 75 × 112 mm, 2,976 cc. High-tension magneto, overhead valves, 100 bhp.
Transmission: 4-speed, shaft drive. 90 mph.
Chassis: Channel-steel, 4-wheel brakes. 9 ft 6 in wheelbase.
Events Won: 1931 Brooklands Double 12 Hour Race (3-litre class), 1931 Brooklands 500 Mile Race (3-litre class).

1932 Bugatti
Type 55 sports car

The Type 55 was the most sporting Bugatti of the 1930s, and combined the 2.3-litre engine of the racing Type 51 with the chassis of another racing model, the Type 54. Most Type 55s carried simple open two-seater bodywork of the type illustrated, but a few closed cars were also made. Despite its good performance, the Type 55 was not prominent in competitions. A total of thirty-eight were made between 1932 and 1935.

Engine: 8-cyl, 60×100 mm, 2,270 cc. High-tension magneto, overhead valves operated by twin ohc, 135 bhp.
Transmission: 4-speed, shaft drive. 112 mph.
Chassis: Channel-steel, 4-wheel brakes. 9 ft wheelbase.

1934 Alfa Romeo
B-2900 Grand Prix racing car

In 1931 Alfa Romeo launched a racing car known as the 8C-2300 or Monza, with 2.3-litre straight-8 engine and two-seater bodywork. The next year the engine was bored out to a capacity of 2.6 litres, and a single-seater was built, known as the B-2600. This has often incorrectly been called the P3. It was extremely successful in 1933, and for 1934 it was followed by the B-2900, another fine car. Unfortunately this had to compete with the new German Grand Prix cars which were substantially state aided, so Alfa's record in 1934 is not so good.

Engine: 8-cyl, 68×100 mm, 2,905 cc. High-tension magneto, overhead valves operated by twin ohc, 210 bhp, twin Roots superchargers.
Transmission: 4-speed, shaft drive. 145 mph.
Chassis: Channel-steel, 4-wheel brakes. 8 ft 10½ in wheelbase.
Events Won: 1934 French Grand Prix, 1934 Monaco Grand Prix, 1934 Targa Florio, 1935 German Grand Prix.

1933 MG
K3 Magnette racing car

The production MG Magnette was intended as a basis for competition activities in the 1,100 cc class. The saloon was known as the K1, the two-seater sports as the K2, and the supercharged sports racing model as the K3. This could be had either with road equipment, in which form one competed in the 1933 Monte Carlo Rally, or as a racing car as illustrated. The latter was driven by the great Italian Tazio Nuvolari to victory in the Tourist Trophy, and was also successful in hill climbs.

Engine: 6-cyl, 57×71 mm, 1,087 cc. High-tension magneto, overhead valves operated by single ohc, 120 bhp.
Transmission: 4-speed, shaft drive. 125 mph.
Chassis: Channel-steel, 4-wheel brakes. 7 ft 10¼ in wheelbase.
Events Won: 1933 Coppa Acerbo, 1933 Tourist Trophy.

1933 Maserati
8CM Grand Prix racing car

The Maserati 8CM was one of the firm's most successful racing cars, and was a worthy rival to the Alfa Romeo B-2600 and 2900. It was the first Maserati to have single-seater bodywork, and also the first with hydraulic brakes. Among prominent drivers of this model were Sir Henry Birkin, Giuseppe Campari, and, in 1934 Tazio Nuvolari and Philippe Etancelin. The photograph shows Etancelin in his privately owned 1933 car at Montlhery in 1934.

Engine: 8-cyl, 69×100 mm, 2,992 cc. High-tension magneto, overhead valves operated by twin ohc, 220 bhp, Roots supercharger.
Transmission: 4-speed, shaft drive. 155 mph.
Chassis: Channel-steel, 4-wheel brakes. 8 ft 4¾ in wheelbase.
Events Won: 1933 French Grand Prix, 1933 Belgian Grand Prix, 1933 Coppa Ciano, 1933 Nice Grand Prix.

1935   Frazer Nash
TT Replica sports car

The Frazer Nash was one of the most individual sports cars ever made, for it retained the chain-and-dog clutch transmission which had been used on its predecessor, the GN cyclecar. Frazer Nashes deserved the title Sports Car more than any of their contemporaries, for comfort was always secondary to performance. Nevertheless, they inspired fierce loyalty among owners, and this is continued today by the Frazer Nash section of the Vintage Sports Car Club. Although transmissions were the same, a variety of engines were used in Frazer Nashes of the 1930s, including Anzani, Meadows, Gough and Blackburne.

Engine: 6-cyl, 60×97.9 mm, 1,657 cc. High-tension magneto, overhead valves operated by twin ohc, 70 bhp.
Transmission: 4-speed, chain drive. 87 mph.
Chassis: Channel-steel, 4-wheel brakes. 9 ft wheelbase.

1935 Mercedes-Benz
W25 Grand Prix racing car

In 1934 a new era of motor racing began with the arrival on the scene of the works teams of Mercedes-Benz and Auto Union cars, both teams backed by the Nazi government who saw motor racing as a valuable means to national prestige. The W25 was the first Mercedes model, and had a twin-ohc supercharged straight-8 engine with four valves per cylinder. It had all-round independent suspension. In late 1934 and 1935 larger engines were used, of 3,720 cc (M25AB), 3,990 cc (M25B), and 4,310 cc (M25C), but the car illustrated, although running in the 1935 French GP at Montlhery, had the 1934 engine of 3,360 cc. Caracciola is at the wheel.

Engine: 8-cyl, 78×88 mm, 3,360 cc. High-tension magneto, overhead valves operated by twin ohc, 354 bhp, Mercedes-type supercharger.
Transmission: 5-speed, shaft drive. 165 mph.
Chassis: Tubular steel, 4-wheel brakes. 8 ft 11 in wheelbase.
Events Won: 1935 French Grand Prix, 1935 Swiss Grand Prix, 1935 Spanish Grand Prix, 1935 Belgian Grand Prix, 1935 Tripoli Grand Prix, 1935 Eifelrennen, 1935 Monaco Grand Prix. (Most of these victories were gained by 4-litre cars.)

1939 BMW

Type 328 sports car

The BMW Type 328 was one of a number of advanced European sports cars which gave the more old-fashioned British cars tough competition in the late 1930s. It had a 6-cylinder engine with inclined overhead valves operated by horizontal pushrods running across the top of the cylinder head to operate the exhaust valves, while the inlets were operated by vertical pushrods in the normal way. Thus only one, side-mounted, camshaft was used. Type 328s took part in a wide variety of races, hill climbs and trials, and a special-bodied coupé won the shortened Mille Miglia in 1940.

Engine: 6-cyl, 66×96 mm, 1,971 cc. Coil, overhead valves, 80 bhp.
Transmission: 4-speed, shaft drive. 95 mph.
Chassis: Tubular steel, 4-wheel brakes. 7 ft 10½ in wheelbase.
Events Won: 1940 Mille Miglia.

1935 Riley
Imp sports car

The Imp was a direct descendant of the original Riley Nine, using a Nine engine in a new short chassis introduced in 1934. It did not compete in the major sports car races such as the Tourist Trophy which were by now the preserve of the larger-engined Rileys, but was widely used by private owners in club races and rallies. A 1,486 cc 6-cylinder engine was also used in this model, when it was known as the MPH Six, but fewer of these were made than of the Imp.

Engine: 4-cyl, 60.3×95.2 mm, 1,089 cc. High-tension magneto, overhead valves, 50 bhp.

Transmission: 4-speed, shaft drive. 75 mph.

Chassis: Channel-steel, 4-wheel brakes. 7 ft 6 in wheelbase.

1934 ERA

racing car

English Racing Automobiles was formed in 1934 by Raymond Mays and Peter Berthon, with financial backing from Humphrey Cook, with the intention of building a British racing car capable of taking on international competition. They did not aspire to Grand Prix level, but aimed at the smaller voiturette class, in which they were very successful. The basis for the ERA's engine was a 6-cylinder 1½-litre Riley, and a simple single-seater body was provided. Suspension was by conventional semi-elliptic leaf springs on all except the 1939 E-type, and this was the least successful of the ERAs. The photograph shows the prototype.

Engine: 6-cyl, 57.5×95.2 mm, 1,488 cc. High-tension magneto, overhead valves, 150 bhp, Jamieson—Roots supercharger.

Transmission: 4-speed, shaft drive. 125 mph.

Chassis: Channel-steel, 4-wheel brakes. 8 ft wheelbase.

Events Won: 1934, 1935 Nuffield Trophy, Donington Park, 1935 Eifelrennen, 1935 Coppa Acerbo, 1935 Masaryk Grand Prix, 1935 Prix de Berne.

DUNLOP

1938 Austin
Seven racing car

The racing cars of 1936 to 1939 were the ultimate development of the racing Austin Seven which had begun in 1923. They had twin overhead camshaft engines with superchargers designed by Murray Jamieson, which revved up to 9,000 rpm. The works cars were driven by Charlie Dodson and H. L. Hadley (seen here at the Crystal Palace), and a side-valve car with similar body was driven by Mrs Kay Petre.

Engine: 4-cyl, 60.3×65.1 mm, 744 cc. High-tension magneto, overhead valves operated by twin ohc, 116 bhp, Jamieson–Roots supercharger.
Transmission: 4-speed, shaft drive. 125 mph.
Chassis: Channel-steel, 4-wheel brakes. 6 ft 10 in wheelbase.
Events Won: 1938 British Empire Trophy, Donington, 1939 Imperial Trophy.

1938 Auto Union
Grand Prix racing car

Auto Union was a combine of four makes of German car who were chosen to be one of the two teams to put German motor racing on the map, shortly after Hitler came to power. Their car was a revolutionary one, designed by Ferdinand Porsche, with engine mounted behind the driver and four wheel independent suspension. The 1934 to 1937 cars had V-16 engines, but for the 3-litre Formula of 1938 Auto Union built a V-12 with three overhead camshafts and de Dion rear suspension.
Engine: 12-cyl, 65×75 mm, 2,990 cc. High-tension magneto, overhead valves operated by 3 ohc, 400 bhp, 2-stage Roots supercharger.
Transmission: 5-speed, shaft drive. 185 mph.
Chassis: Tubular steel, 4-wheel brakes. 9 ft 4 in wheelbase.
Events Won: 1938 Italian Grand Prix, 1938 Donington Grand Prix, 1939 Yugoslav Grand Prix, 1939 French Grand Prix.

1946 Novi

Special racing car

Introduced in 1941, the Novi Specials were unusual among Indianapolis cars in that they used their own design of engine, whereas most competitors from the mid-thirties to the mid-sixties relied on the 4-cylinder Offenhauser power unit. The Novi was a more sophisticated engine, being a 3-litre V-8 with two camshafts to each bank, and a centrifugal supercharger. For a long time, Novis were the fastest cars at Indianapolis, but they suffered many breakdowns, often spectacular, and never won the 500 Mile Race.

Engine: 8-cyl, 80.2×66.7 mm, 2,726 cc. Coil, centrifugal supercharger.
Transmission: 2-speed, shaft drive. 190 mph.
Chassis: Tubular, 4-wheel brakes. 8 ft wheelbase.

1950 Alfa Romeo
Tipo 159 Grand Prix racing car

Alfa Romeo's post-war Grand Prix car was designed in 1938 for the voiturette races in which it did very well. After the war its 1½-litre supercharged engine made it eligible for the new Grand Prix formula, and it had a long string of successes from 1946 to 1951. The 1950 model was called the Tipo 159 and the 1951 the Tipo 159A. By this time the engine was developing over 400 bhp at 10,500 rpm, compared with 190 bhp at 6,500 rpm from the original 1938 engine. Farina became the first World Championship Driver in 1950 in a Tipo 159, and Fangio repeated this achievement in 1951.

Engine: 8-cyl, 58×70 mm, 1,479 cc. High-tension magneto, overhead valves operated by twin ohc, 335 bhp, Roots supercharger.

Transmission: 4-speed, shaft drive. 175 mph.

Chassis: Tubular, 4-wheel brakes. 8 ft 2 in wheelbase.

Events Won: 1950 Belgian Grand Prix, 1950 French Grand Prix, 1950 Monaco Grand Prix, 1950 British Grand Prix, 1950 Italian Grand Prix, 1950 Swiss Grand Prix.

1948 Ferrari
125 Grand Prix racing car

This car was one of the first series of cars to be called Ferrari, the other two being sports cars. It appeared after them, making its début in the 1948 Italian GP when Raymond Sommer drove one to 2nd place. The car's first victory came later in the year at Garda, and in 1949 Ferraris won three Grands Prix. However, that year Alfa Romeo virtually withdrew from racing, and the 1½-litre Ferraris were not competing against Alfa's Tipo 159s. In 1950, when the Alfas returned, Ferrari turned to building 4½-litre unsupercharged cars.

Engine: 12-cyl, 55×52.5 mm, 1,498 cc. Magneto, overhead valves operated by twin ohc, 225 bhp (300 in 1949), single supercharger (2-stage in 1949).
Transmission: 5-speed, shaft drive. 170 mph.
Chassis: Tubular, 4-wheel brakes. 7 ft 1 in wheelbase.
Events Won: 1948 Garda Grand Prix, 1949 Swiss Grand Prix, 1949 Italian Grand Prix, 1949 Dutch Grand Prix.

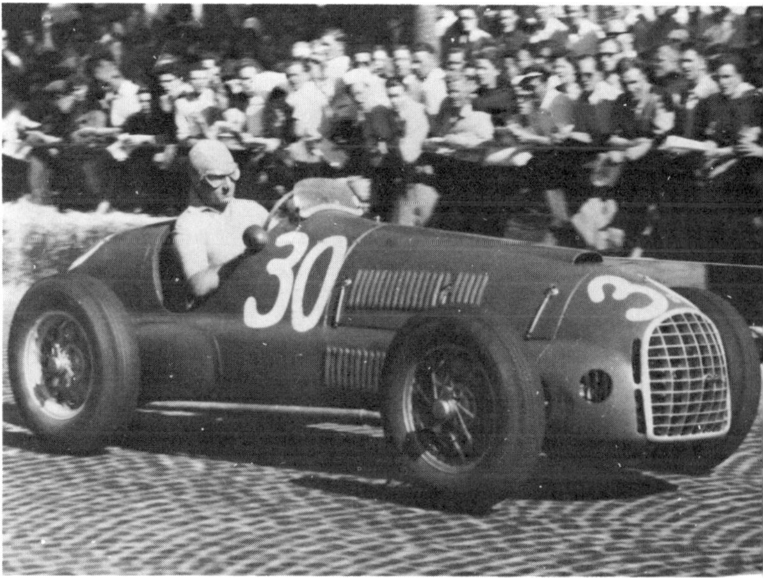

1948 Simca Gordini
racing car

Amedée Gordini was an engineer who began tuning French Simca cars before the war, having considerable success in the *Bol d'Or* races. In 1946 he designed his first single-seaters for Simca, still using the Fiat-based 1,100 cc engine. This was enlarged to 1,220 cc in 1947 and to 1,433 cc in 1948. In the latter form the Simca Gordini developed 105 bhp and had a number of successes in minor events. Without a supercharger they could not compete with Grand Prix cars such as Ferrari or Alfa Romeo. Gordini tried a supercharger on a 1950 car, but it was unsuccessful, and the unblown single-seaters continued until 1951, when Gordini left Simca to become a manufacturer in his own right.

Engine: 4-cyl, 78×75 mm, 1,433 cc. High-tension magneto, overhead valves, 105 bhp.
Transmission: 4-speed, shaft drive. 130 mph.
Chassis: Tubular steel, 4-wheel brakes.
Events Won: 1948 Perpignan Grand Prix, 1948 Angoulême Grand Prix, 1948 Stockholm Grand Prix.

1949 MG
TC Midget sports car

The TC Midget was a development of the very similar TB which was introduced in April 1939. Large numbers were exported in the post-war years, especially to the United States where it sparked off a sports car revival. The TC's performance was not startling, but its sporty appearance and low lines earned it many enthusiasts. By 1949 it was distinctly old fashioned, and in 1950 it was replaced by the TD which had independent front suspension.

Engine: 4-cyl, 66.5×90 mm, 1,250 cc. Coil, overhead valves, 55 bhp.
Transmission: Shaft drive. 78 mph.
Chassis: Channel-steel, 4-wheel brakes. 7 ft 10 in wheelbase.

1949 Ferrari
166 sports car

The Ferrari 166 was derived from the first series of sports cars, and is thus a cousin to the 125 Grand Prix car. Its engine was enlarged from 1½ litres to 2 litres in capacity, and for 1949 a new style of body was adopted, designed by Superleggera Touring and called the Barchetta. It was with one of these that Luigi Chinetti and Lord Selsdon won the first post-war Le Mans 24 Hour Race, the first of Ferrari's ten victories to date in this event.

Engine: 12-cyl, 60×58.8 mm, 1,995 cc. Coil, overhead valves operated by twin ohc, 140 bhp.
Transmission: 5-speed, shaft drive. 136 mph.
Chassis: Tubular steel, 4-wheel brakes. 7 ft 2½ in wheelbase.
Events Won: 1949 Le Mans 24 Hour Race, 1949 Mille Miglia, 1949 Spa 24 Hour Race.

1950 Cooper
Mark IV Formula 3 racing car

Charles Cooper and his son John were among the architects of Formula 3, and in fact built their first 500 cc car four years before the Formula was first recognized by the FIA in 1950. Engines used were all motorcycle units, at first JAP and later 'double-knocker' twin-ohc Norton. Stirling Moss achieved his first victories in a Cooper 500, and among other drivers who began their careers on the little Coopers were Peter Collins, Ivor Bueb and Stuart Lewis-Evans.

Engine: 1-cyl, 79×100 mm, 499 cc. High-tension magneto, overhead valves operated by twin ohc, 45 bhp.

Transmission: 4-speed, chain drive. 120 mph.

Chassis: Box-section steel, 4-wheel brakes. 7 ft 1 in wheelbase.

1950 Jaguar
XK120 sports car

The Jaguar XK120 was one of the most sensational cars of its day, with its beautiful lines and excellent performance. Some sceptics doubted that it could be a 120 mph car, but one was timed at 132.6 mph on a motorway in Belgium, and ordinary customers' cars were capable of 124 mph. The XK120 also showed Sir William Lyons' remarkable capacity for making first class cars at reasonable prices; when it came out, the XK120 cost only £1,263. Of the 7,500 made up to 1954, less than 10% were sold in Britain, all the rest went abroad. A drop-head coupé and fixed-head coupé were added to the range, but the classic model was always the open two-seater.

Engine: 6-cyl, 83×106 mm, 3,442 cc. Coil, overhead valves operated by twin ohc, 160 bhp.

Transmission: 4-speed, shaft drive. 125 mph.

Chassis: Channel-steel, 4-wheel brakes. 8 ft 6 in wheelbase.

Events Won: 1950 Tourist Trophy, 1950 and 1951 Silverstone Production Car Race.

1952 BRM
Grand Prix racing car

The BRM was conceived by Raymond Mays as a national racing car to compete with the best that the Continent could offer, and was financed by a large number of firms in the industry. The first car had a V-16 supercharged engine running up to 11,000 rpm, and the makers had high hopes of it when it was demonstrated late in 1949. However, a variety of troubles plagued the cars during 1950 and 1951, and the following year the project was bought by the industrialist Alfred Owen. The $1\frac{1}{2}$-litre cars were raced spasmodically for three more years but were never really successful, and in 1955 a new 4-cylinder car was built for the $2\frac{1}{2}$-litre formula.

Engine: 16-cyl, 49.53×47.8 mm, 1,496 cc. High-tension magneto, overhead valves operated by 4 ohc, 430 bhp, 2-stage Rolls-Royce supercharger.
Transmission: 5-speed, shaft drive. 185 mph.
Chassis: Tubular steel, 4-wheel brakes. 8 ft 2 in wheelbase.
Events Won: 1952 Daily Graphic Trophy, Goodwood, 1952 Woodcote Cup, Goodwood, 1953 Glover Trophy, 1953 Charterhall Formule Libre Race, 1953 Snetterton Formule Libre Race.

1951 Allard
J2 sports car

Sydney Allard built a few Ford-engined sports cars before the war, but did not go into proper production until 1946, again using Ford engines in cars of striking appearance. In 1949 the lightweight sports car J2 appeared, powered by Ford engines for the British market, but for America they were exported without engines, to be fitted with Cadillac or Lincoln power units. Among successful drivers of Cadillac–Allards was Tom Cole who won at Bridgehampton in 1950, and with Sydney Allard was 3rd at Le Mans the same year. The photograph shows Sydney Allard in a Cadillac-engined J2 at Goodwood.

Engine: 8-cyl, 96.83 × 92.07 mm, 5,420 cc. Coil, overhead valves, 170 bhp.

Transmission: 3-speed, shaft drive. 115 mph.

Chassis: Channel-steel, 4-wheel brakes. 8 ft 4 in wheelbase.

Events Won: Pebble Beach (California) Sports Car Race, Bridgehampton (Long Island) Sports Car Race.

1951 Dellow

sports car

The Dellow was designed specifically as a trials car, and was the best-known of three makes of trials car which were factory-produced. It was powered by a Ford Ten engine and optional extras included twin carburettors and a supercharger. Later Dellows could be had with the Ford Consul engine. Production lasted from 1949 to 1956 when the design illustrated was replaced by an all-enveloping fibreglass body of which very few were made.

Engine: 4-cyl, 63.5×92.5 mm, 1,172 cc. Coil, side valves, 37 bhp, optional Wade–Roots supercharger.

Transmission: 3-speed, shaft drive. 70 mph.

Chassis: Tubular, 4-wheel brakes. 7 ft 6 in wheelbase.

1954 Mercedes-Benz
W196 Grand Prix racing car

After fifteen years' absence, Mercedes-Benz returned to the Grand Prix scene in 1954 with the W196, an advanced racing car with a $2\frac{1}{2}$-litre straight-8 engine using desmodromic valve gear and fuel injection. Other features of the design included 5-speed gearboxes, inboard brakes and a streamlined body which made the W196 look more like a sports car than a Grand Prix contender. In the form shown it won the French GP, but later cars used a more conventional open-wheeled body. The Mercedes team had a spectacular 1955 season with the W196, winning the Drivers' and Manufacturers' Championships, and then withdrew at the height of their success. Mercedes have not been seen in Grand Prix racing since.

Engine: 8-cyl, 76×68.8 mm, 2,496 cc. Coil, overhead valves operated by twin ohc, 290 bhp.
Transmission: 5-speed, shaft drive. 175 mph.
Chassis: Space-frame, 4-wheel brakes. 7 ft $8\frac{1}{2}$ in wheelbase.
Events Won: 1954 French Grand Prix (Streamlined car), 1954 German Grand Prix (Open-wheel car), 1954 Swiss Grand Prix, 1954 Italian Grand Prix.

1953 Triumph

TR2 sports car

In the early 1950s there was no British sports car in the medium price and performance class between, say, the MG Midget on one hand and Jaguar or Aston Martin on the other. The Triumph TR2 was intended to bridge this gap, and it was very successful. The engine was a slightly reduced version of the Standard Vanguard which was in mass production at the time, while front suspension, rear axle and chassis frame came from other Standard or Triumph cars. This enabled the price to be kept down to £871, and yet the TR2 was capable of over 100 mph. It was replaced in 1956 by the TR3.

Engine: 4-cyl, 83×92 mm, 1,991 cc. Coil, overhead valves, 90 bhp.

Transmission: 4-speed, shaft drive. 104 mph.

Chassis: Channel-steel, 4-wheel brakes. 7 ft 4 in wheelbase.

1951 Cunningham

sports car

Briggs Cunningham was a wealthy American enthusiast who dreamed of seeing an American victory at Le Mans. In 1950 he entered two Cadillac-engined cars (one a standard sedan) which finished 10th and 11th, and the following year he built two sports cars with Chrysler engines, tubular frames and de Dion rear axles. Although one car was in 2nd place for some time, they did not finish at all high in the list. Cunninghams ran at Le Mans each year until 1955, their best placing being 3rd in 1953 and 1954.

Engine: 8-cyl, 96.83×92.07 mm, 5,420 cc. Coil, overhead valves, 220 bhp.
Transmission: 4-speed, shaft drive. 130 mph.
Chassis: Tubular steel, 4-wheel brakes. 8 ft 9 in wheelbase.
Events Won: 1953 Sebring 12 Hour Race.

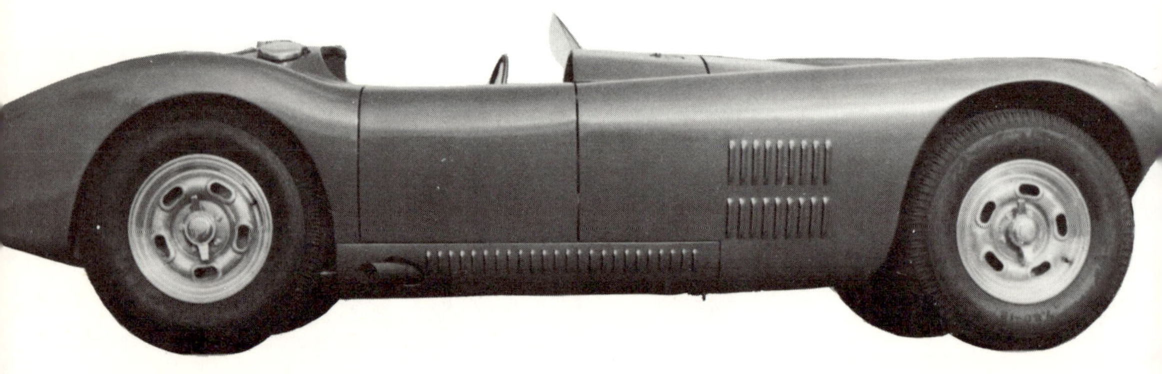

1953   Kurtis
Indianapolis racing car

Frank Kurtis built his first racing cars in the early 1930s, concentrating on midgets until after World War II. He then turned to building cars for Indianapolis, these included the chassis of the winning cars in 1950, 1951, 1953, 1954 and 1955. The engines of all these cars were Offenhausers. Kurtis also built the chassis for the Novi cars and a number of sports cars. His total production of Indianapolis cars was fifty-eight, while midgets amounted to over 800, not including those sold in kit form.

Engine: 4-cyl, 102×114 mm, 4,123 cc. Coil, overhead valves operated by twin ohc.
Transmission: 2-speed, shaft drive. 180 mph.
Chassis: Tubular steel, 4-wheel brakes. 8 ft wheelbase.
Events Won: 1953 Indianapolis 500 Mile Race.

1954 Jaguar
D-type sports car

The first specifically competition Jaguar was the C-type, derived from the production XK120, which won the Le Mans 24 Hour Race in 1951, and again in 1953. For 1954 Jaguar engineer William Heynes developed a new sports/racing car with monocoque construction and 250 bhp engine. This was the D-type which finished 1st, 2nd and 3rd in the Rheims 12 Hour Race, although it had to be content with 2nd place at Le Mans. However, later versions of the D-type won at Le Mans in 1955, 1956 and 1957. A number of replicas were sold to private owners, but a road-equipped version known as the XK-SS did not go into production.
Engine: 6-cyl, 83×106 mm, 3,442 cc. Coil, overhead valves operated by twin ohc, 250 bhp. **Transmission**: 4-speed, shaft drive. 195 mph. **Chassis**: Monocoque, 4-wheel brakes. 7 ft 6 in wheelbase. **Events Won**: 1954 and 1956 Rheims 12 Hour Race, 1955, 1956 and 1957 Le Mans 24 Hour Race, 1955 Ulster Trophy.

1956 Aston Martin
DBR-1 sports car

The DBR series marked the beginning of Aston Martin's new programme of sports/racing car development, with more divergence from the standard road-going cars than ever before. A new twin overhead camshaft 6-cylinder engine was used, with dry sump lubrication, multi-tubular frame and five-speed gearbox. The DBR-1 was first seen in action at Le Mans where it retired, and the new cars did not meet with great success until 1957 when 3-litre models won the Spa Sports Car GP and the Nürburgring 1,000 Kilometres race. In 1959 Aston Martin won the Sports Car Championship with a 3-litre DBR-1/300, which was a direct development of the car illustrated.
Engine: 6-cyl, 2,493 cc. Coil, overhead valves operated by twin ohc, 260 bhp.
Transmission: 5-speed, shaft drive.
Chassis: Tubular steel, 4-wheel brakes. 7 ft 6 in wheelbase.

1956 Maserati
250F Grand Prix racing car

The 250F was the most successful Maserati of the post-war period, and enabled Fangio to win the 1957 World Championship and Stirling Moss to be runner-up in 1956. It was a relatively simple design, the work of Gioacchino Colombo, with 6-cylinder twin overhead camshaft engine, tubular space frame and de Dion rear axle. They were sold to private owners as well as being raced by the works, and a total of thirty-two were built between 1954 and 1958, a very large production figure for a Grand Prix car.

Engine: 6-cyl, 84×75 mm, 2,494 cc. High-tension magneto, overhead valves operated by twin ohc, 270 bhp.
Transmission: 5-speed, shaft drive. 165 mph.
Chassis: 4-wheel brakes. 7 ft 5 in wheelbase.
Events Won: 1956 Richmond Trophy, Goodwood, 1956 BARC 200 Mile Race, 1956 and 1957 Monaco Grand Prix, 1956 Italian Grand Prix, 1957 Argentine Grand Prix, 1957 French Grand Prix, 1957 German Grand Prix, 1957 Morocco Grand Prix.

1954   Lancia
D50 Grand Prix racing car

The D50 represented the first ever attempt by the old-established Lancia company to enter Grand Prix racing. It had a 2½-litre V-8 engine and a five-speed gearbox, together with the distinctive feature of pannier fuel tanks occupying the space between front and rear wheels. Their first season was unsuccessful, but in 1955 they did well with drivers of the calibre of Ascari, Villoresi and Castelotti. Tragically, Ascari was killed while testing a sports Ferrari at Monza, and this combined with financial troubles, forced Lancia out of Grand Prix racing.

The cars were sold to Ferrari who raced them under the name Lancia-Ferrari in 1956 and 1957.
Engine: 8-cyl, 73.6 × 73.1 mm, 2,489 cc. High-tension magneto, overhead valves operated by 4 ohc, 260 bhp.
Transmission: 5-speed, shaft drive. 170 mph.
Chassis: Tubular spaceframe, 4-wheel brakes. 7 ft 6 in wheelbase.
Events Won: 1955 Turin Grand Prix, 1955 Naples Grand Prix.

1958 Vanwall
Grand Prix racing car

In 1954 the industrialist Tony Vandervell decided to run a team of Grand Prix cars of his own, which he named Vanwall, from *Van*dervell and Thin*wall*, the name of the shell-bearings which were widely used in racing car engines. The Vanwall had an entirely new engine designed by Leo Kuswicki and was built in the Norton racing department. The original 1954 engine had a capacity of 2 litres, but this was enlarged to 2½ litres in 1955, and in 1956 the Frank Costin-designed body was adopted. In 1958 Vanwall won the Formula One Manufacturers' Championship, with three victories each by Stirling Moss and Tony Brooks. The latter is seen here winning the German GP at the Nürburgring.

Engine: 4-cyl, 96×86 mm, 2,490 cc. Overhead valves operated by twin ohc, 285 bhp.
Transmission: 5-speed, shaft drive. 175 mph.
Chassis: Tubular spaceframe, 4-wheel brakes. 7 ft 6½ in wheelbase.
Events Won: Dutch Grand Prix, Portuguese Grand Prix, Moroccan Grand Prix, Belgian Grand Prix, German Grand Prix, Italian Grand Prix.

1956 Lotus
11 sports car

The first Lotus sports car to have an aerodynamic body was the Mark 8 of 1954, followed by the generally similar Mark 9 and Mark 10 with a variety of engine options. In 1956 came the Mark 11 illustrated, which was one of the most successful of the series. It had a complex space frame, body designed by Frank Costin, and the option of Ford or Coventry-Climax engines, the latter canted at an angle of 10° from the vertical. Reg Bicknell and Peter Jopp won the 1,100 cc class at Le Mans in 1956, and in 1957 a Lotus 11 with 744 cc engine won the Index of Performance at Le Mans. Later cars with similar bodies were the Mark 15 and Mark 17, usually with 1½- or 2-litre engines.

Engine: 4-cyl, 72.4×66.6 mm, 1,098 cc. Coil, overhead valves operated by twin ohc.
Transmission: 4-speed, shaft drive.
Chassis: Tubular space frame, 4-wheel brakes. 7 ft 4 in wheelbase.

1957   DB
sports coupé

France built few large sports cars in the 1950s, but instead a large crop of small cars based on family saloons appeared, and contested major events such as Le Mans with great success. Among these was the DB (Deutsch et Bonnet), which used the 610 cc air-cooled flat-twin engine from the Dyna Panhard saloon. It first appeared in 1948, but from the early 1950s the larger 745 cc engine was used, and the make had many successes with both open and closed cars. Most remarkable of these was outright victory in the 1954 Tourist Trophy race, but DB also won the Index of Performance at Le Mans five times between 1954 and 1961. The photograph shows a 745 cc coupé which ran at Le Mans in 1957.

Engine: 2-cyl, 72×75 mm, 745 cc. Coil, overhead valves, 39 bhp.
Transmission: 4-speed, shaft drive. 90 mph.
Chassis: Channel-steel, 4-wheel brakes, 8 ft 5$\frac{1}{4}$ in wheelbase.

1957 Ferrari
315MM

After a series of 4- and 6-cylinder sports cars, Enzo Ferrari returned to the V-12 layout with the Tipo 290MM, designed by Vittorio Jano who had been responsible for the pre-war Alfa Romeo sports and racing cars. The V-12s were much more successful than the 1955 6-cylinder cars had been. The Tipo 315MM illustrated was the enlarged version raced in 1957.

Engine: 12-cyl, 76×69.5 mm, 3,780 cc. Coil, overhead valves operated by 4 ohc, 380 bhp.

Transmission: 4-speed, shaft drive. 190 mph.

Chassis: Tubular steel, 4-wheel brakes. 7 ft 8½ in wheelbase.

Events Won: 1957 Mille Miglia.

1958 Salih
racing car

After Frank Kurtis retired from the manufacture of Indianapolis cars, two new names came to the fore, A. J. Watson and George Salih. Both still used the traditional Offenhauser engine, but Salih achieved a lower line than any of his contemporaries by laying the engine almost flat on its side. These cars were known as 'lay-down roadsters', and were seen at Indianapolis until the end of the front-engined era in the mid-sixties. The photograph shows Jimmy Bryan in the Salih car with which he won the 1958 500 Mile Race.

Engine: 4-cyl, 102×114 mm, 4,123 cc Coil, overhead valves operated by twin ohc.
Transmission: 2-speed, shaft drive. 180 mph.
Chassis: Tubular spaceframe, 4-wheel brakes. 8 ft wheelbase.
Events Won: 1958 Indianapolis 500 Mile Race.

1959 Cooper

Grand Prix racing car

The Formula One Cooper had its origin in a rear-engined centre-seat sports car built in 1955, which was raced in Formula Two form in 1957 and 1958, while in 1959 the engine was enlarged to nearly 2½ litres, bringing it into the Formula One category. In the hands of Stirling Moss and Maurice Trintignant, Coopers had already won two Grands Prix in 1958, and the next year Jack Brabham won the World Driver's Championship. This firmly established the rear-engined racing car as the future pattern, and very soon all racing cars carried their engines behind the driver.

Engine: 4-cyl, 94×89.9 mm, 2,495 cc. Coil, overhead valves operated by twin ohc, 240 bhp.
Transmission: 5-speed, transaxle. 160 mph.
Chassis: Tubular steel, 4-wheel brakes. 7 ft 7 in wheelbase.
Events Won: 1959 New Zealand Grand Prix, 1959 Monaco Grand Prix, 1959 British Grand Prix, 1959 Portuguese Grand Prix, 1959 Italian Grand Prix, 1959 US Grand Prix.

1958 Giaur
racing car

Formula Junior began in Italy as a national class for 1,100 cc cars using production engines, in practice nearly always Fiats. Among the many constructors were the partners Domenico Giannini and Bernardo Taraschi who had built sports cars under the name Giaur since 1950, and produced the Formula Junior car illustrated in 1958. The following year a more streamlined body reminiscent of the Vanwall was adopted, and the name changed to Taraschi.

Engine: 4-cyl, 68×75 mm, 1,089 cc. Coil, overhead valves.
Transmission: 4-speed, shaft drive. 100 mph.
Chassis: Tubular, 4-wheel brakes.

1960 Chevrolet
Corvette sports car

The Corvette was introduced in 1953 and was at that time a good-looking but not particularly sporting car with a 3.7-litre 6-cylinder engine developing 150 bhp. A V-8 engine came in 1955, and the following year Chevrolet engineer Zora Arkus-Duntov began to develop the car into a race winner. Fuel injection and a four-speed manual gearbox became available in 1957, and although General Motors would not support Duntov's hopes of entering Corvettes at Le Mans, they achieved many successes in American events. In 1960 Briggs Cunningham took two cars to Le Mans, where they finished 8th and 10th. The car driven by John Fitch and Bob Grossman is seen here at the start.

Engine: 8-cyl, 98.4×76 mm, 4,637 cc. Coil, overhead valves, 300 bhp.
Transmission: 4-speed, shaft drive. 160 mph.
Chassis: Box section, 4-wheel brakes. 8 ft 6 in wheelbase.

1961 Maserati
Tipo 61 sports car

Maserati did not support sports car racing with a works team after 1957, but they continued to build cars for private owners to buy. From 1959 to 1961 they made a series of cars which came to be known as the Birdcage Maseratis, because of the very complex space frame construction. The Tipo 60 had a 2-litre engine canted at an angle of 45°, and Stirling Moss won the Rouen Sports Car Race with it. It was followed by the generally similar Tipo 61 (illustrated) which had a 2.9-litre engine. It was fast but fragile, and had few significant victories apart from those listed. In 1961 came the rear-engined Tipo 63, but this was even less successful.

Engine: 4-cyl, 100×92 mm, 2,890 cc. Coil, overhead valves operated by twin ohc, 250 bhp.

Transmission: 5-speed, shaft drive. 170 mph.

Chassis: Tubular spaceframe, 4-wheel brakes. 7 ft 2½ in wheelbase.

Events Won: 1960 Cuban Grand Prix. 1960 and 1961 Nürburgring 1,000 Km Race.

1965 Cobra
sports coupé

The original Cobra combined the excellent independently sprung chassis of the English AC Ace with an American Ford V-8 engine, but many improvements were made at the suggestion of the American racing driver Carroll Shelby, so that by 1965 the cars were much more American than British. A 4.7-litre 380 bhp Ford engine was used in the team cars which Shelby raced with great success in 1964 and 1965, winning the GT Championship in both years. The Daytona coupé illustrated was a special works team car, and could not be bought by the public.

Engine: 8-cyl, 101.6×73 mm, 4,727 cc. Coil, overhead valves, 350 bhp.
Transmission: 4-speed, shaft drive. 185 mph.
Chassis: Tubular steel, 4-wheel brakes. 7 ft 6 in wheelbase.
Events Won: 1965 International GT Championship.

1962 BRM

V-8 Formula 1 racing car

BRM turned to rear-engined cars in 1960 with a 2½-litre machine, and in 1961, having no 1½-litre engine of their own ready, used a 4-cylinder Coventry-Climax unit. For 1962 they introduced their 1½-litre V-8 engine, and this gave the make the first really striking successes they had ever enjoyed. In this they were greatly helped by the driving of Graham Hill, who won his first World Championship for himself, and also the Constructors' Championship for BRM.

Engine: 8-cyl, 68.5×50.8 mm, 1,498 cc. Coil, overhead valves operated by 4 ohc, 200 bhp.

Transmission: 6-speed, transaxle. 190 mph.

Chassis: Monocoque central, tubular front and rear sections, 4-wheel brakes. 7 ft 6 in wheelbase.

Events Won: 1962 Glover Trophy, Goodwood, 1962 Daily Express Trophy, Silverstone, 1962 Dutch Grand Prix, 1962 German Grand Prix, 1962 SA Grand Prix.

1963 Lotus
Indianapolis racing car

This car had as much influence on American racing as the original rear-engined Cooper had on world racing car design. Known as the Mark 29, it had a 4.2-litre Ford V-8 engine in a typical Lotus chassis, and Jim Clark drove it into 2nd place at Indianapolis, to the amazement of the Indy 'Establishment', who had used the traditional front-engined Offenhauser-powered roadsters for nearly twenty years. Two years later Clark was back again with the monocoque Lotus 38, and this time he won. Since then, American builders have all turned to rear-engined cars, and the Indianapolis car is much closer in appearance to its European counterpart.

Engine: 8-cyl, 96×73 mm, 4,261 cc. Coil, overhead valves operated by 4 ohc, 365 bhp.
Transmission: 4-speed, transaxle. 190 mph.
Chassis: Monocoque, 4-wheel brakes. 8 ft wheelbase.

1964 Porsche
Carrera 904 sports car

In the development of Porsche cars from the road-going Type 356 of the 1950s to the ultra-fast Type 917, the car illustrated marked an important step forward. It was the first to use a fibreglass body, and also the first closed Porsche to adopt the mid-position of the engine, behind the driver but ahead of the rear axle. As well as the racing successes listed below, the Carrera 904 came second in the 1965 Monte Carlo Rally, a most unusual achievement for such a low-slung, basically racing, car.

Engine: 4-cyl, 92×74 mm, 1,966 cc. Coil, overhead valves operated by 4 ohc, 180 bhp.
Transmission: 5-speed, transaxle. 165 mph.
Chassis: Box section, 4-wheel brakes. 7 ft 6¾ in wheelbase.
Events Won: 1964 Targa Florio.

1966 Ford
GT40 sports coupé

Ford decided to enter sports car racing in 1963, and chose to develop the Lola coupé with Ford engine which Eric Broadley had just completed. The first Ford GT40 (so called because the roof line was exactly 40 inches from the ground), used the same 4.2-litre V-8 engine that Broadley's Lola had, but a larger 4.7-litre engine was soon adopted, and in the Mark 2 of 1965 onwards Ford's largest V-8 of 7 litres was used. Success was slow, nothing to show in 1964, and little in 1965. However, in 1966 the Mark 2s won at Le Mans, Daytona and Sebring, and later developments of the GT40 theme, raced by Ford up to 1967 and J. W. Automotive thereafter, had further Le Mans victories in 1967, 1968 and 1969.

Engine: 8-cyl, 108×96 mm, 6,997 cc. Coil, overhead valves, 475 bhp.
Transmission: 4-speed, transaxle. 210 mph.
Chassis: Monocoque, 4-wheel brakes. 7 ft 11 in wheelbase.
Events Won: 1966 Daytona 24 Hour Race, 1966 Sebring 12 Hour Race, 1966 Le Mans 24 Hour Race.

1965 Austin-Healey
3000 sports car

The Austin-Healey had its origin in a sports car called the Healey Hundred which was exhibited at the 1952 London Motor Show. It was powered by a 2.6-litre 4-cylinder Austin engine, and before the Show was over Sir Leonard Lord of Austin's had arranged for it to be made by his firm instead of at the little Healey works, and it was re-named the Austin-Healey. It became one of Britain's most popular sports cars and was made, with many changes, until 1968. Most important of the changes was the introduction of a 2.6-litre 6-cylinder engine in 1956, which was enlarged to 3 litres in 1959. The car illustrated is taking part in the 1965 RAC Rally of Great Britain, its crew being Timo Makinen and Paul Easter.

Engine: 6-cyl, 83.36×89 mm, 2,912 cc. Coil, overhead valves, 150 bhp.
Transmission: 4-speed, shaft drive.
Chassis: Channel-steel, 4-wheel brakes. 7 ft 8 in wheelbase.

1966 Brabham
BT20 Formula 1 racing car

The first Formula 1 Brabhams of 1962 used the $1\frac{1}{2}$-litre Coventry-Climax V-8 engine, but for the new 3-litre Formula of 1966 Jack Brabham and his chief engineer Ron Tauranac used the Australian Repco V-8 with only one camshaft per bank of cylinders. These cars were slower than some of their rivals, but their reliability helped Jack Brabham to win the World Championship in 1966, a feat which Denny Hulme repeated the following year.

Engine: 8-cyl, 88.9 × 60.3 mm, 2,994 cc. Coil, overhead valves operated by twin ohc, 285 bhp.
Transmission: 5-speed, transaxle. 185 mph.
Chassis: Tubular spaceframe, 4-wheel brakes. 7 ft 8 in wheelbase.
Events Won: 1966 French Grand Prix, 1966 British Grand Prix, 1966 Dutch Grand Prix, 1966 and 1967 German Grand Prix, 1967 Monaco Grand Prix.

1966 Matra-BRM
2-litre sports/racing car

The French aerospace and missile engineering firm of Matra entered the motor racing world when they acquired the sports car firm of Réné Bonnet in 1964. They built Formula 3 cars in 1965, and for Le Mans in 1966 entered a team of three of the coupés illustrated, powered by the 2-litre V-8 BRM engine. They were heavy and not particularly successful, but they were followed by further sports cars powered by Matra's own 3-litre V-12 engine. A development of this, with open bodywork, won at Le Mans in 1972.

Engine: 8-cyl, 73.28×59.18 mm, 1,998 cc. Coil, overhead valves operated by 4 ohc, 275 bhp.
Transmission: 5-speed, transaxle.
Chassis: Space frame, 4-wheel brakes.

1967 Chapparal
2F coupé

Chapparal cars were built in Texas by racing driver Jim Hall from 1962 to 1970. It was a private venture, no cars being sold by Hall, but the small concern turned out some highly unconventional and successful cars. They pioneered the use of adjustable aerofoils at the rear of the car, aimed at improving road adhesion during cornering, this feature being clearly visible in the photograph of a Chapparal 2F in the Targa Florio. Another unusual feature of most Chapparals was automatic transmission. Hall's cars were only seen in European sports car racing for two seasons, 1966 and 1967, as their Chevrolet engines were too large for the 1968 3-litre regulations, but they competed regularly in Can Am events.

Engine: 8-cyl, 107×95.5 mm, 6,997 cc. Coil, overhead valves, 525 bhp.
Transmission: Automatic, shaft drive. 215 mph.
Chassis: Monocoque fibreglass, 4-wheel brakes.
Events Won: 1967 Brands Hatch 500 Mile Race.

1966 Lola

T70 Mark 2 sports/racing car

After Eric Broadley left Ford where he had collaborated on the GT40 cars, he recommenced manufacture of his own Lola cars at Slough, and in 1965 built the first of the T70 series, large sports/racing cars powered by Chevrolet V-8 engines. The 1965 cars had steel monocoque construction, but in 1966 aluminium was used for the central section. John Surtees won that year's Can Am Series in a T70 Mark 2. Later, in 1967, a coupé was introduced, the Mark 3B, which was the most successful of the series. The photograph shows Denny Hulme driving a Mark 2 to victory in the 1966 Tourist Trophy at Oulton Park.

Engine: 8-cyl, 6,300 cc. Coil, overhead valves.
Transmission: 5-speed, transaxle. 200 mph.
Chassis: Monocoque steel, 4-wheel brakes. 7 ft 11 in wheelbase.
Events Won: 1966 Guards Trophy, Brands Hatch, 1966 Players Quebec, 1966 Los Angeles Times Grand Prix, 1966 Stardust Grand Prix.

1969 Porsche
917 coupé

Porsche had become increasingly a make to be reckoned with in sports car racing in the 1960s, and the 917 was their largest contender. It had a flat-twelve engine developing 520 bhp at 8,000 rpm, and in order to qualify it for Group 4 the company built an initial series of twenty-five cars, offering them for sale at over £14,000. The handling of the early 917s was not good, and they had only one small success in their first year. In 1970 the cars were run by the J W Automotive team who had previously raced the Ford GT, and also by the Austrian Porsche company. The improved 917s had an excellent season, winning the Sports Car Constructors' Championship, a feat which they repeated in 1971.

Engine: 12-cyl, 85×66 mm, 4,494 cc. Coil, overhead valves operated by 4 ohc, 520 bhp.

Transmission: 5-speed, transaxle. 230 mph.

Chassis: Tubular spaceframe, 4-wheel brakes. 7 ft 6 in wheelbase.

Events Won: 1970 Daytona 24 Hour Race, 1970 BOAC 500 Km Race, 1970 Monza 1,000 Km Race, 1970 Spa 1,000 Km Race, 1970 Le Mans 24 Hour Race, 1970 Watkins Glen 6 Hours Race, 1970 Oesterreichring 1,000 Km Race.

1969 STP Oil Treatment Special
Indianapolis racing car

This car is typical of the new generation of Indianapolis racing cars, many of which are derived from European designs. In the case of the STP, the inspiration came from Brabham, although the car was designed by Clint Brawner. The engine was a special Ford unit which was supercharged, and could turn at a maximum of 10,800 rpm. Mario Andretti drove the car to victory at Indianapolis at a record speed of 156.867 mph.

Engine: 8-cyl, 91 × 48.2 mm, 2,605 cc. Coil, overhead valves operated by 4 ohc, 650 bhp, Schwitzer turbocharger.
Transmission: 4-speed, transaxle. 190 mph.
Chassis: Monocoque, 4-wheel brakes. 8 ft 2½ in wheelbase.
Events Won: 1969 Indianapolis 500 Mile Race.

DUNLOP
4
elf

1969   Matra
MS80 Formula 1 racing car

Matra's first Formula 1 car of 1967 used their own make of V-12 engine, but the Englishman Ken Tyrrell preferred to use the Cosworth V-8 engine in his team of Matra cars. The 1968 MS2 used this engine in a much-modified Formula 2 chassis, and with this car Jackie Stewart was runner-up in that year's World Championship. For 1969 there appeared the MS80, with the same engine in a new chassis, and with this car Stewart won his first World Championship, and the first Grand Prix Championship ever for a French car, albeit one with an English engine and a Scottish driver.

Engine: 8-cyl, 85.6×64.8 mm, 2,993 cc. Coil, overhead valves, operated by 4 ohc, 430 bhp.
Transmission: 5-speed, transaxle. 190 mph.
Chassis: Monocoque, 4-wheel brakes. 7 ft 10½ in wheelbase.
Events Won: 1969 SA Grand Prix, 1969 Spanish Grand Prix, 1969 Dutch Grand Prix, 1969 British Grand Prix, 1969 German Grand Prix, 1969 Italian Grand Prix.

1969   Matich
SR4 Group 7 racing car

Frank Matich was one of Australia's most successful drivers, when he turned to the construction of cars in 1965. He has built fewer than ten, all large Group 7 machines powered by American V-8 engines, an Oldsmobile in the first, and latterly Chevrolet. Matich cars have raced successfully not only in Australia and New Zealand, but also in Can Am events in the United States.

Engine: 8-cyl, 460 bhp.
Chassis: 7 ft $7\frac{3}{4}$ in wheelbase.
Max. Speed: 195 mph.

1970 Mallock
U2 Clubman's racing car

Since the Clubman's Formula began in 1965 one of the most successful constructors has been Arthur Mallock whose simple, reasonably priced cars have taken numerous championships, including the 1965 and 1968 Clubman's Championship and 1969 Formula 1200 Championship. Engines used have been mostly BMC and Ford units of up to 1,600 cc, and the cars are built in either two-seater form for Formula 1200 or Clubman work, or as single-seaters for Formula Ford. The latter are the only front-engined machines to compete in this Formula, but still manage to give a good account of themselves.

Engine: 4-cyl, 80.96×77.62 mm, 1,599 cc. Coil, overhead valves.
Transmission: 4-speed, shaft drive.
Chassis: Tubular, 4-wheel brakes.

1970 Royale
RP4 Formula F100 and RP3 Formula Ford cars

The small North London firm, Racing Preparations Ltd, were the most successful builders of cars for the F100 Formula, a two-seat Formula Ford with cars which looked rather like scaled-down Can Am machines. Ray Allen won the 1970 F100 Championship with a Royale RP4 similar to the car on the left of the photo. The other Royale is a Formula Ford car which has achieved numerous successes in both Britain and the United States, where over 90% of the production was sold.

Engine: 4-cyl, 80.96×77.62 mm, 1,599 cc. Coil, overhead valves, 100 bhp.
Transmission: 4-speed, shaft drive. 115 mph.
Chassis: Spaceframe, 4-wheel brakes. 7 ft 7 in wheelbase.
Events Won: 1970 USA Formula Ford Championship.

1971 McLaren
M8E Group 7 racing car

The name McLaren has become synony-mous with Can Am racing, the cars from Slough winning practically every event in the series from 1967 to 1970, though recently they have faced stiffer opposition from their rivals, Porsche in particular. There has been a steady line of develop-ment from the first Group 7 McLaren-Oldsmobile of 1965 through to the M8E illustrated, the latter Chevrolet-powered like all Group 7 McLarens since 1967.

Engine: 8-cyl, 107×95.5 mm, 6,997 cc. Coil, overhead valves, 625 bhp.
Transmission: 4-speed, transaxle. 200 mph.
Chassis: Monocoque, 4-wheel brakes 7 ft 10 in wheelbase.

1970   Ferrari

512S sports/racing car

For 1970 Ferrari followed Porsche's lead in building a large-engined car with which to contest the sports car championship. As the maximum limit for prototypes was 3 litres, Ferrari's 5-litre 512S had to be built in a series of at least twenty-five, like Porsche's 917. The Italian cars were less successful than their rivals, however, and won only one Championship race, Sebring, although they were second many times.
Engine: 12-cyl, 87×70 mm, 4,994 cc. Overhead valves operated by 4 ohc, 580 bhp.
Transmission: 5-speed, transaxle. 220 mph.
Chassis: Monocoque, 4-wheel brakes. 7 ft 10½ in wheelbase.
Events Won: 1970 Sebring 12 Hour Race, 1970 Kyalami 9 Hour Race.

1971 Alfa Romeo
33 sports/racing car

The Tipo 33 series marked a return to serious motor racing for the Alfa Romeo company who had built no team cars since the mid-1950s. The Tipo 33 first appeared in 1967 with a 2-litre V-8 engine in a tubular chassis and with a coupé body, but many changes have been made since then. The engine was increased to 2½ litres in 1968 and to 3 litres in 1970, while the tubular chassis was replaced by a riveted duralumin platform chassis in 1970. Open as well as closed models have been made. While they have never dominated sports car racing, the Tipo 33s have had a number of satisfying wins, including Nino Vacarella's in the 1971 Targa Florio (seen here in the photo).

Engine: 8-cyl, 78×66 mm, 2,990 cc. Coil, overhead valves operated by 4 ohc, 300 bhp.
Transmission: 6-speed, transaxle. 210 mph.
Chassis: Platform, 4-wheel brakes. 7 ft 4 in wheelbase.
Events Won: 1971 Targa Florio.

1972 Chevron

BT21 sports/racing car

The Bolton-based Chevron company have been highly successful with 2-litre sports/racing cars, starting with their B3 coupés
of 1966. Later cars had BMW, Coventry-Climax or Cosworth
engines, while the first open sports car, the B19, appeared in
1970. The B21 illustrated is a development of this, available
with Cosworth FVC or EA engines.
Engine: (Cosworth EA) 4-cyl, 88.9×80.3 mm, 1,994 cc.
Overhead valves operated by twin ohc, 265 bhp.
Transmission: 5-speed, transaxle.
Chassis: Semi-monocoque aluminium, 4-wheel brakes.
7 ft 9 in wheelbase.

1972 Lola
T300 Formula 5000 racing car

Lola have been among the most successful builders of Formula 5000 cars, virtually Formula 1 machines with large American V-8 engines of up to 5 litres capacity. One of the leading Lola drivers was Frank Gardner who made a number of suggestions about improving the design of the 1969 cars, and was taken on as a member of Lola's development staff. He won the 1971 Rothmans Formula 5000 Championship, partly with the T192 and partly with the new T300 which he had helped to develop. This car, the 1972 version of which is illustrated, had side-mounted radiators.

Engine: 8-cyl, 101.7×76.2 mm, 4,942 cc. Transistorized, overhead valves, 400 bhp.
Transmission: 5-speed, transaxle. 170 mph.
Chassis: Monocoque, 4-wheel brakes. 8 ft 5 in wheelbase.

1972 Tyrrell
005 Formula One racing car

Ken Tyrrell was a successful entrant of racing cars who joined the ranks of the constructors in mid-1970 when he announced a conventional Cosworth-engined Formula One car for Jackie Stewart to drive as an alternative to the March car which Tyrrell had been entering since the beginning of the season. Two cars were used in 1971, driven by Stewart (who won the Championship) and François Cevert. The 1972 season was started with 1971 cars, but a new model with inboard front brakes and side-mounted oil radiators appeared at the French Grand Prix. This was the 005, illustrated in practice for the Italian Grand Prix, with Stewart at the wheel. With it the Scotsman had two convincing victories late in the season, in the Canadian and US Grands Prix.

Engine: 8-cyl, 85.6×64.8 mm, 2,993 cc. Transistorized, overhead valves operated by 4 ohc, 440 bhp.

Transmission: 5-speed, transaxle. 185 mph.

Chassis: Monocoque, 4-wheel brakes. 7 ft 10½ in wheelbase.

Events Won: 1972 Canadian Grand Prix, USA Grand Prix.